When

Grief

Descends

Suffering, Consolation, And The Book Of Job

Anne Mackie Morelli

B.PE, M.A., R.C.C.

Kristi –
"In his hands is
the life of every living
thing and the breath of
every human being" – Job 12:10

Thanks for liking me up
with Todd + Kyra + your worthiness.
to meet over coffee + talk writing
+ books + for reviewing this book.
I appreciate it all –
Blessings Anne Mackie Morelli

As You Wish Publishing, LLC Connect@asyouwishpublishing.com

ISBN-13: 978-1-951131-03-6
Library Of Congress Control Number: 2020909322

Edited by Todd Schaefer

Printed in the United States of America.

Nothing in this book or any affiliations with this book is a substitute for medical or psychological help. If you are needing help please seek it.

All Bible references are from the New Revised Standard Version (NRSV) translation unless otherwise noted.

Endorsements

Anne Mackie Morelli is a clinical counsellor with many years of training, experience, and accrued wisdom. This book does well to explain the differences between cognitive and emotional grief reactions. Anne discusses what to do and when to do it. Unfortunately, as Anne describes, grief and mourning are not linear. There is not a formula provided or a direct line to take us from the beginning to the end or finish line. Grief is the process of mourning a loss. This book explains the issues and concerns involved with comforting a sufferer.

The first chapter, *My Winter Season,* will make you cry. Anne exposes personal incidents of grief and suffering. I read this chapter twice, put the book down, and waited a while to read the rest. Having said that, the rest of the book is certainly worth reading. Anne explains what the Book of Job reveals about suffering in such a way that a layperson will understand, and a scholar will appreciate the analyses.

Anne's book, *When Grief Descends,* makes a major contribution to this area of counselling. Anne's writing is excellent, but her insights are the most powerful part. Thanks, Anne, for writing this book and putting yourself out there for everyone to see.

Dr. John Carter, Ph.D., Psychologist
University of British Columbia, Teaching Associate

Up until now, *Job* has been one of my least favourite books of the Bible. Anne Mackie Morelli's beautifully written book, which draws on the expertise of both biblical scholars and counsellors, has changed that. The author takes us through Job's grieving process and, from his example and that of his friends, she highlights practical and timeless ways we can help those who are grieving, including ourselves. Anne also briefly explores Job's journey of re-evaluating his simplistic and inadequate theology of suffering. *When Grief Descends* has reaffirmed my love for Scripture, and it has better prepared me for times of loss and grief that come to each one of us. This book is full of valuable, useful information that I know will make me a better friend.

Marg Mowczko, M.A., B.Th,
Writer, https://margmowczko.com/

This is a timely book. "Whenever adversity is unpredictable and unexpected, it can feel as though God is just being capricious, indifferent or unjust." Why does God let suffering happen? Anne's vulnerability and wisdom breathe hope. Whether you are in a winter season that seems dark and accompanied with deep suffering, or in the spring and experiencing renewed joy and hope, this book will speak to your moment. As we face, wrestle, embrace and sit with grief, the pages of this book hold golden gems on how to be a better friend, an authentic believer in Yahweh, a gracious companion in good times and in bad.

Anne Miranda, Pastor of Women's Ministries,
Village Church, Langley, British Columbia, Canada

I have been privileged to read Anne Mackie Morelli's body of work on the Book of Job. While many author's focus on what Job's suffering is, Anne looks at what Job's suffering can teach us about distress and about coming alongside to comfort. The lessons on interpreting suffering and enhancing comforting are rooted in the timeless truth that to live is to suffer. Readers will learn to understand the complexities of loss and grief, and they will be encouraged to develop a Christian theology of suffering. Such understandings will support the development of practical skills to navigate suffering so as to become a consoling comforter.

Anne points out that as reflected in the life and sorrow of Job, reactions encompass emotional, cognitive, spiritual and physical parts of one's being. Yet, as Anne reminds us, God is in the narrative of the griever, even when the griever feels abandoned. Job's narrative invites us into the assurance that God has been ever-present and listening. As Anne has learned from her own life sorrows, God will be with us "even when we are sitting on the ash heaps of our own lives."

Anne lives and writes the testimony of her words "God broke into my story," calling, trusting, waiting restoring and transforming. Transforming life and action so that she has now become a consoling comforter. As an instructor of those who will offer comfort to the sorrowing, I look forward to being able to use this volume as required reading for ministry students.

Gloria J. Woodland, D.Min
Chaplaincy Program Director,
ACTS Seminaries, Trinity Western University

Grief has a way of entering our lives unannounced. Anne Mackie Morelli's book, *When Grief Descends*, will prepare you for the unexpected twists in life and give you the tools you need to understand the grief process. Anne's writing will soothe your soul and strengthen your ability to skillfully comfort your friends and family during times of loss. Not only does Anne give permission to grieve, but she also helps us understand the unique emotional journey we may face.

Anne displays raw vulnerability as she weaves in her personal story of stumbling through grief and turning to the Bible for comfort. Anne weaves in lessons from the Book of Job, reminding us that it is okay to rest in discomfort and feel authentically. In a world where positivity is glorified, Anne grounds us and reminds us it is okay to struggle. *When Grief Descends* will strengthen your ability to comfort others and will renew your faith. If you have lost your way, this book will bring you home.

Kristi Blakeway, B.Ed, M.A.
Principal, Author of *Beyond Hello*

This is an immensely practical field guide and toolbox. Using Job's story as the backdrop, Mackie Morelli gives us tools to learn the language and terrain of grief. She teaches us what to expect when considering the contours of this unfamiliar and unwelcome landscape. And yet, she is careful to note that the trajectory of grief is different for each one of us. She also equips us to comfort the grieving instead of adding insult to their injury. If we heed Morelli's wisdom and guidance, we'll avoid being the kind of miserable and clumsy comforters Job's friends were. May we do so!

Marlena Graves, M.Div
Author, *The Way Up Is Down: Finding Yourself by Forgetting Yourself*

While we seek to erase, hide, and skip over our grief, Anne invites us to take a seat and really observe it—to face our long-held beliefs about how we should grieve as Christians and how we show up for ourselves and others in times of great loss. Using the story of Job as a practical and spiritual lens, Anne thoughtfully guides her readers to reflect and apply what they have read to further cement the concepts and tools she shares. Most of all, Anne's willingness to expose the wounds of her grief to hold her readers up is both beautiful and heart-breaking, begging this book to be read again and again as an evergreen resource for anyone who has suffered loss of any scale. What a timely message for our world.

Quantrilla Ard, Ph.D. M.Ph,
Writer, The Ph.D. Mama

Author Anne Mackie Morelli wrote *When Grief Descends* with three goals for her readers: to begin developing a Christian theology of suffering, to understand loss and grief, and to learn how better to console others in their suffering. Her book beautifully succeeds in all three areas by offering a careful study of the book of Job, reflecting on her own deep experiences of loss, and drawing on the expertise of others. This excellent resource is biblically grounded, well-researched, and wise, with plenty of practical examples, plus exercises for readers to try for themselves. I recommend *When Grief Descends* for both individuals and churches seeking to grow in compassion and caring.

April Yamasaki, Pastor and Author of *Sacred Pauses: Spiritual Practices for Personal Renewal* and *Four Gifts: Seeking Self-Care for Heart, Soul, Mind, and Strength*

The Book of Job—that little book tucked away in the Old Testament that we either avoid or gloss over during our Bible devotionals. We generally dismiss it as "outdated" or "not relevant" to today's society. In her book, *When Grief Descends: Suffering, Consolation and The Book Of Job*, Anne Mackie Morelli blows those theories right out of the water. By allowing us to witness not only the suffering of Job but her own deeply personal seasons of loss and grief, Anne leads us down the path to a better understanding of loss and the grieving process. Her book is not only a Divine-inspired interpretation of the Book of Job, but also a textbook of the grieving process designed to offer comfort to those who are grieving, and those who desire to become "consoling comforters" to those who are suffering.

When Grief Descends is a practical and useful guide for understanding and dealing with the day-to-day realities of grief and suffering. Each chapter ends with an opportunity to reflect on the information given as well as apply that information to one's personal situation. Utilizing her vast knowledge and experience in the counselling and education fields, Anne Mackie Morelli has included a wealth of guidelines, resources and practical applications for anyone dealing with their own grief or that of others in the community.

When Grief Descends is uplifting and inspiring and provides much-needed light for the dark seasons of our lives.

Shirlyn Evans, M.Ed, University of New Mexico
Reading Specialist

When Grief Descends, as the title evokes, the book abounds with stimulating ideas and questions: practical and well-tested insights. Inspired by her own family journey and personal experience, Anne Mackie Morelli, with her deep faith in God, boldly shares with the reader a well-researched and balanced analysis showing that in suffering, we can find meaning, including fulfillment in God. The author challenges the reader and provides wisdom on how the "comforter" should approach the "sufferer" with respect and dignity. I highly recommend this book and wish it a global readership.

Phocas Ngendahayo, M.A. Rwanda Country Director Abundant Leadership Institute Foundation

Over the past 30 years, not only have I experienced significant personal grief, I have walked alongside a countless number of people in theirs. My experiences have taught me that in this cultural moment, we are most interested in comfort and pleasure, and therefore ill-equipped to respond when pain and grief come.

Through the lens of scripture, Anne helps us shape healthy expectations around personal pain, disappointment, and loss, and equips us with tools for having important conversations with others about suffering and comforting those in need.

Cliff Ursel, Pastor, Westside Church, Vancouver, B.C.

In *When Grief Descends*, Anne Mackie Morelli has woven together insightful and well-researched observations from the Job narrative, her own deep experiences of suffering, best practices from the field of counselling, and her expertise as a registered clinical counsellor into a profound and engaging look at how anyone can grow as a theologically-informed and skillful consoling comforter.

Dr. Randy Wolff, Associate Professor of Practical Theology and Leadership Studies at ACTS Seminaries and Director of the ACTS World Campus (Online Seminary)

As a former teacher, administrator, track & field coach and life-long friend of Anne Mackie Morelli, it is my privilege and honour to endorse her book as a work of art and a must-read for everyone. Her hard work in her track & field career took her to an Olympic level for Canada, and after reading her book, I would say she has done the same once again with her latest endeavour. Anne's own suffering is what led her to the Book of Job, which in her own words, "can teach us about suffering, stimulate thoughtful reflection and fruitful discussions."

What helps to make this book so interesting, is Anne's comparisons of grief and loss with modern-day events and with those of the early Biblical days with Job. As she says in her book: 'grief is the process of mourning a loss and is unique to each individual.' We can identify with Anne's own experiences as the near loss of her sister, the death of her parents and family health issues which tested her own beliefs, but again have added credibility to her book because she has walked the walk and not just talked the talk when it comes to suffering and loss. Anne's overarching goal is for the reader to understand suffering and how we can become more consoling companions. The Reflections and Applications at the end of each chapter are important as they reinforce what you have read, ask questions that make you think about your own experiences, and provide food for thought. From my point of view and through reading her book, her goals were accomplished. *When Grief Descends* helped me to see myself and how I handle grief. The lessons I learned will make me a better comforter for my family and friends in their time of need.

In closing, I wholeheartedly endorse Anne's book as a must-read, not once but at least twice, as there is so much important information to absorb. I would strongly recommend you buy a copy of her book for a family member or friend. It will be a valuable part of their library and a gift they will thank you for.

Coach Lawrence King, Retired High School Administrator, Calgary, Alberta, Canada

To my beloved ones.

To those who bravely walked into our winter season.

To those who rolled up their sleeves and walked shoulder to shoulder.

To those who were willing to learn and grow with me.

To those who listened and offered grace.

To those who comforted.

To those who supported me through this project and offered wise counsel.

To those who love me and forgive me, in spite of all my stumbles.

And to our unfathomable, beautiful, loving God,

my heart overflows with gratitude.

Table of Contents

Foreword by Dr. Dorothy Peters

Anne Morelli writes out of her profound life as an educator and counsellor, as a student of the Bible and an Olympian, as a mother and wife and daughter and friend. She writes as one acquainted with suffering. An accumulation of losses led her into what she describes as an experience of complex trauma, an "unsettling" for which she was wholly unprepared, with a theology ill-equipped to process suffering.

In the biblical character of Job, Anne encounters a kindred spirit. In Job's companions, she recognizes those who valiantly try to be "consoling comforters" but who suffer from a flawed theology that falters before the hard questions of a lamenting, theologically traumatized Job.

However, as Anne ably observes, even though the conversations between Job and his companions become "heated and combative, they do highlight the importance of being able to process," a process necessary for unearthing the "partial truths that have unconsciously been woven into our belief systems."

In this beautifully and sensitively written book, readers are invited into an intimate and vulnerable journey with Anne and with the character of Job as conversation partners. Counsellors, biblical scholars and writers also come alongside as she leads all into a timeless and cross-cultural "listening," a masterful weaving of theological and counselling perspectives. At just the right moments, Jesus-the-sufferer speaks, highlighting the profound shift in ways the conversation of suffering developed into the New Testament.

There are many delightfully insightful observations that mutually illuminate counselling and theological perspectives. One of my favourite examples is the observation that Job's "laments are often incoherent, erratic, and irrational." Anne writes:

"When we ... look at Job's grief we can see that it was not a linear or orderly progression. Job's thoughts were jumbled, disordered and conflicted, and circled back and around. At one moment, Job spoke with confidence about God's goodness and justice. Then in the next moment, he lamented with despair and confusion about God's injustice, before looping back to praise God."

Whereas biblical scholars have often struggled with how to interpret Job's non-linear expressions of confidence followed by despair, praise, lament, Anne notes Job's jumble of thoughts and emotion as typical to grief. Seen from a counselling perspective, therefore, the ordering of Job's speeches throughout the book is illuminated and made sensible.

Is the character of Job one meets in this book intended to be a time-traveling "client" to a professional counsellor, the subject of a case study, an object of biblical interpretation, or simply a friend? Are readers meant to become better counsellors, better biblical interpreters, or simply better-consoling comforters?

I would say that the answer is "All of this and more." We also find ourselves as one in the midst of suffering and questioning humanity. The book works well as inspirational reading for the individual or as a conversational centerpiece for group therapy or Bible study groups.

Finally, as a postscript, one must not neglect the appendices! Some of the most powerfully practical moments are buried in the back of the book where readers traverse time and culture to sit with Job as his companions, guided into asking questions and offering responses that open the way for consolation and comfort.

Dorothy M. Peters, Ph.D.
Adjunct Professor
Trinity Western University and ACTS Seminaries

Foreword by Louise Roberts

I was hesitant when Anne asked me to read her book and write a foreword for it.

How could the Book of Job offer comfort? It is difficult to read. Full of pain and suffering. Uneasy and uncomfortable.

And Anne's strong faith and her theological background vary greatly from my own. But then I realized that what mattered was how committed we both have been in joining with people as they've worked through their distress. How easily we have bounced ideas and co-written teaching content for school counselling professionals and how our opinions have always meshed.

Then, when I began to read her book, I was thrilled.

Anne fearlessly jumps in. Her vulnerability in sharing her own stories of loss raises her writing to above the ordinary. It is Anne's personal journey that helps connect Job's narrative and her beliefs. We begin to understand how her faith supported her in her own suffering season, and where others may find succour for themselves, or to offer to others.

The information Anne shares in her book is vital as our society shifts and changes, where we are less able to lean into our families and fewer feel the support of our communities. Loss, however, is a universal truth. We all experience loss.

I see many uses for the information Anne has shared. Few people have the knowledge or experience with how to help someone in pain. Anne furnishes us with her faith, her guidance and her research. With every chapter, she asks us to reflect on the things we are reading and how we are processing them. Anne shows us how we can support and console, rather than run from distress and misery.

This book can be used individually by someone wanting to work through their own grief reactions. Paid church professionals (pastor, minister, priests or elders) who may feel unequipped to help but see the need in their congregation could work through Anne's book and acquire skills that would help them to provide comfort to others in their suffering. Congregations that are active, who encourage guided study and other spiritual groups such as grief care or care and compassion teams but see loss and grief as an area that has been misunderstood, now have a blueprint. Counsellors who offer guidance for loss and grief but would like to consolidate their faith-based approach now have the opportunity to become more informed. Book clubs and community groups could read it and work through it as a study. And university professors, who teach chaplaincy and spiritual care classes, could use this book as a required textbook.

There is enough theological substance to satisfy the most discerning and learned scholar. Anne's references range far, and they underpin her discussions on her faith and her belief in the power of Job's narrative to offer healing. Anne is very clear about what she believes—that her faith and belief in God have the power to provide solace and comfort in the midst of overwhelming pain. With well-considered questions, pertinent Appendices, and a reading list, Anne makes practising basic skills and processing how one feels seem accessible, and we are guided through this journey.

Anne also makes a few important things very clear. In order to wade into another's grief, we need to take an honest accounting of where we are at—and offer only what we are capable of giving. This capacity will ebb and flow as our own lives change. Next, she highlights how important it is to be well-grounded in our own understanding and bias around faith and loss and grief. Ensuring that each of us understands where our personal beliefs merge and differ from what we have been taught about faith and religion, and loss and grief.

Finally, and most importantly, Anne reminds us that grief is not a theological problem that mere words can solve. We must be careful not to judge or force our ideas or bias on others. Rather, we are invited to be vulnerable, to provide a safe presence, to listen and share, and to show our hearts. Only then will we become capable of providing healing solace.

Louise V Roberts, B.Sc., M.Sc. (Psychology)
Retired Clinical Counsellor

"Now when Job's three friends heard of all these troubles that had come upon him, each of them set out from his home- Eliphaz the Temanite, Bildad the Shuhite, and Zophar the Naamathite. They met together to go and console and comfort him."

- Job 2:11 (New Revised Standard Version)

"Then Job defended himself: 'I've had all I can take of your talk. What a bunch of miserable comforters! Is there no end to your windbag speeches? What's your problem that you go on and on like this? If you were in my shoes, I could talk just like you. I could put together a terrific harangue and really let you have it. But I'd never do that. I'd console and comfort, make things better, not worse!'"

- Job 16:1-5 (The Message)

Chapter One
My Winter Season

"You made me like a handcrafted piece of pottery – and now you are going to smash me to pieces? Don't you remember how beautifully you worked my clay? Will you reduce me now to a mud pie?...You gave me life itself, and incredible love. You watched and guarded every breath I took. But you never told me about this part. I should have known there was more to it..."Job 10:8-9, 12-13. The Message

Life was good. We were thriving as we walked through a long season of prosperity. That's not to say that everything was smooth or easy for us, for we had certainly faced challenges. But overall, we'd been able to overcome any hurdles with relative ease. As a result, my partner and I had slipped into a sense of complacency and self-sufficiency.

Then all of a sudden, a series of major losses shattered our season of prosperity, and we were catapulted into a season of suffering.

I often think of this time as being something like what people must have experienced when the Titanic, a large luxury cruise ship, crashed into an iceberg and sank. Without warning or time to prepare, the passengers found themselves tossed into the dark and frigid waters. One moment they were seated in the luxurious dining room or having a casual evening stroll on the promenade deck, and the next moment they found themselves in the dark night, floundering in the surging waves.

When Grief Descends

Over a six-year period, crisis after crisis derailed the trajectory of our lives. We faced several major losses, including the deaths of my father and mother, my mother-in-law and sister-in-law. Some family members were diagnosed with chronic illnesses such as Crohn's disease, cancer, Parkinson's, fibromyalgia, dementia, arterial sclerosis, mental health and post-traumatic stress disorders, and multiple sclerosis. Other family members contended with abandonment issues and broken hearts.

Even our physical spaces were invaded when one of the two major rivers that flow through the city of Calgary, Alberta, erupted over its banks and ravaged an entire section of the city. My mother's home of 55 years was one of the thousands of homes and businesses that were heavily flooded. She lost everything in her basement, including treasured family photos and personal files. Shortly after this, the basement of our own home flooded when a drainage pipe became clogged. Finally, my physical health was compromised when I began to struggle with chronic back pain and fibromyalgia.

At first glance, this list of our losses may bear a resemblance to any typical list that you or I might compose on a daily basis. Perhaps it reads analogous to the way a grocery list or a to-do list reads, where we list the items we need to buy or the things that need to get done. But in reality, a list of such losses can never be read in such a superficial, inconsequential way. This kind of list is just not that simple. For each loss represents an acute, distinctive loss that has its own particular breadth and depth and nuance of pain. With distress that had to be faced and walked into, worked through and processed.

As our losses accumulated, my grief shifted into complex trauma. Oftentimes, the grief was suffocating. It felt like I had to struggle to draw the next breath. Even little worries could trigger my anxiety. It was always more noticeable at night when silence blanketed our home. Apprehension prowled around and pressed in. Because sleep was often elusive, I'd end up sleeping with my Bible on my chest. Or, I'd visualize myself curling up by Jesus's feet, in part hidden by his flowing robe. Or grabbing onto the hem of his robe and not letting him go. Then comfort would come to find me and offer me sleep.

Our winter was a brutal season. Not just because of all the losses we had to face, but because I was caught off guard. I was unprepared to face that volume of loss and grief. Without realizing it, I had allowed the post-Christian secular culture, with its entitlement, materialism, false-promises, cynicism, and deception to influence my thinking and how I saw the world. This is an earthly economy built on the constructs of reward and punishment, the idea that good people deserve to be rewarded, and wicked people deserve to suffer. It is a quid pro quo structure, where things are logical, everything adds up, what is fair is fair, and people get what they deserve. It is a view that is so pervasive and insidious, so crafty and subtle; it had seeped into the way I was framing and living my life.

It unsettled me to be so unprepared, especially because I am an educator and a registered clinical counsellor who had spent my entire professional career counselling and teaching in high school and community settings. I had always been willing to take on challenging assignments and enter into hard stories of loss. Early in my career, I worked in a community counselling center in a remote northern community and provided art and play therapy to children as young as five, all of whom had been sexually or physically abused or neglected. Later, I worked as a counsellor in an alternative school setting for high school students who had exhausted all other regular school options because of their chronic non-attendance, defiance, non-compliance, violence, or substance abuse. I facilitated parenting groups for women who had had their children apprehended because of neglectful or abusive parenting. I worked with teens who had been kicked out of their homes and teens who struggled with depression and suicidal ideation. I was on the school district's crisis response team, which supported schools whenever they faced events like the death of a student or a violent episode. I worked with individuals, couples and families as they struggled with anger, conflict, relationship and substance abuse issues, and faced loss and grief. I had entered into the spaces of suffering to sit with the broken.

Yet, very early in our winter season, I learned that even though I *knew about* loss and grief and how to console others, I did not *know* it. All my knowledge and experience had remained at an objective, cognitive level of understanding. But now, as I entered into my own season of suffering, this head knowledge was about to be integrated at a subjective, heart level.

Our adversity also challenged my faith. I quickly discovered how ill-equipped I was to process my suffering through the lens of my Christian faith. But then, I providentially stumbled into the Book of Job. This book of the Bible focuses on the main character, Job, his narrative of tragic losses, overwhelming grief, and his struggle to understand how a good God fit into his suffering. Immediately, his narrative resonated with me. Although Job was righteous, he too had suddenly experienced a series of catastrophic losses that launched him into overwhelming grief, a re-examination of his theology, and his eventual restoration. (See Appendix A for a brief *Summary of The Book of Job.*)

Job ascribed to the reward and retribution theology, where the righteous earned and deserved their prosperity, and the wicked were punished. But, when he was faced with adversity, including the loss of his ten children, his estate, and his standing in the

4

community, he realized there were some serious flaws to his theology. Carol A. Newsom, Sharon H. Ringe and Jacqueline E. Lapsley address this in their Biblical commentary, *Women's Bible Commentary,* when they write,

> "Without his really being aware of it, his sense of identity, his expectations about the world and his place in it, and even his image of God had all been shaped by his status in a particular social and moral order. When his world is shaken by the suffering he undergoes, it became possible to see something of the dimensions and the dimensions of that world."[1]

Job's plight and his lament stirred my heart. "Remember that you fashioned me like clay; and will you turn me to dust again?" (10:8-9). "Why do the wicked live on, reach old age, and grow mighty in power?" (21:7) "What have I done to deserve this?" (Msg 30:24) "Why have you made me your target? Why have I become a burden to you? Why do you not pardon my transgression and take away my inequity?" (7:20-21). "What is my strength, that I should wait? And what is my end, that I should be patient?" (6:11). And how I wish my companions could become more consoling in my sorrow! (19:1; 13:4; 16:1-2).

His lament articulated the yet unformed and obstructed cries of my own heart. They formed the questions that were just starting to percolate in my own mind. And as I began my grief journey and searched for answers alongside Job, I identified with his confusion and isolation. I also found myself growing impatient with the uncertainty, the not knowing, the lack of control over my life. Just like Job, I struggled to understand and yearned to move past this grinding winter season.

There were also times when my family and friends, who despite having good intentions and genuine desires to care for me, bore a resemblance to Job's "miserable companions" (16:2). Their sincere, but misguided efforts and words only served to complicate my suffering and increase my sense of isolation. And there were times where I was so emotionally drained and spiritually dry that I also struggled to be kind and gentle and patient with others.

After a time, I began to sort through the rubble, searching for meaning. I wanted to understand my suffering through the lens of the Christian faith. I engaged in grief and trauma counselling. I voraciously read books that looked at suffering from a Christian perspective. I continued with my daily devotionals but now sought what the Bible could teach me about hardship, loss and suffering. I enrolled in a seminary program at a local university, and as part of the Master's degree in Christian Studies and Leadership, took classes such as the *Exposition of the Book of Job, Pastoral Care for Grief and Loss*, *Prayer and the Practice of Ministry, Spiritual Formation for Ministry Leaders, Spiritual Care* and *Exposition of the Psalms*, that stretched how I viewed God, the Christian faith and suffering.

As I walked through our winter season, I experienced firsthand how our culture and the church as a whole tend to avoid the hard topics of loss and grief, trauma and suffering. Old Testament theologian and scholar Walter Brueggemann writes about this in his book, *Spirituality of the Psalms*, when he contends,

> "The dominant ideology of our culture is committed to continuity and success and to the avoidance of pain, hurt, and loss. The dominant culture is also resistant to genuine newness and real surprise. It is curious, but true, that

surprise is as unwelcome as is loss. And our culture is organized to prevent the experience of both."[2]

This avoidance of suffering can be evidenced in how few churches provide classes or sermons that specifically focus on loss, trauma, suffering, or how to be a consoling comforter. Few churches seem willing to tackle the biblical books, such as the Book of Job or Lamentations, which are rich resources for forming a Christian understanding of suffering. As a result, believers remain fundamentally unfamiliar with loss and grief and find it difficult to navigate their own suffering or to comfort others.

Nancy Reeves builds on the idea of institutions and individuals avoiding grief, in her book, *Found Through Loss, Healing Stories from Scripture & Everyday Sacredness.* She writes that ignoring loss and grief leads to what she defines as disenfranchised loss and grief, "…a situation where society, religious institutions, or significant individuals in our lives do not acknowledge or allow our grief."[3] When institutions and social networks are unwilling to enter into suffering, it prevents opportunities for the sufferer to share their loss and grief, and it communicates that their loss or pain is unacceptable, not valid or worth acknowledging. She provides some examples of where disenfranchised loss and grief are particularly noticeable, including "miscarriage, abortion, incarceration, children's grief, loss of relationships that are not sanctioned by 'authority' and male grief."[4]

Yet, while the church encourages members to support the sufferer, it seldom offers specific instruction and training offered for their members around how to best provide that pastoral care. So, I began to wonder. What can the contemporary church do to prepare people for the inevitable loss and grief they will face? How can they help to form a robust understanding of suffering? What books and resources are available that can help a sufferer or comforter to navigate grief? In what ways might a church help their people to move from being the miserable companions in Job's narrative, and become more consoling comforters?

In his book, *A Liturgy of Grief. A Pastoral Commentary on Lamentations,* Leslie C. Allen offers one answer. He proposes that churches should start using biblical books that focus on grief, suffering and lament as a way to help their people learn how to embrace the grieving process. He writes,

> "[The Book of Lamentations] validates grief. It is God's gift to those who grieve" and "the intent of the book is to honor human grief; the title invests grief with spiritual value. The book sanctifies the human process of dealing with the consequences of suffering as invaluable to its victims and so to a compassionate God... Grief creates a canon within the biblical canon, headed by the books of Job and Lamentations and the lament psalms in the book of Psalms. They all offer literary companionship... The main thing is that they all embrace grief."[5]

Timothy Keller supports all these ideas when he points out in his book, *Walking with God Through Pain and Suffering*, that this insufficient preparation for suffering contrasts with how one of the main themes in the Bible is suffering.[6] Ellen F. Davis also concurs with Allen and Keller, when she writes in her book, *Getting Involved With God, Rediscovering the Old Testament,*

> "It is safe to say that at the present time, the church makes little use of the Book of Job for its pastoral ministry. This has not always been the case. The medieval church made heavy use of it in preparing Christian souls to deal with

suffering without falling away from their faith. But the modern church has pulled back, even in recent decades." 7

As Timothy Keller aptly points out, the church's reluctance to candidly deal with loss and grief diverges from what Scripture reveals about God, trials and suffering. Through God's written Word, and specifically in the Book of Job, it is clear that God is very aware of human suffering. He is present in our suffering, and he grieves on our behalf. He suffers when we sin and turn away from him.8

Jesus is intimately familiar with human suffering. He personally experienced rejection, mockery, humiliation, loss, minimization, exclusion, ridicule, persecution, abuse, torture and an excruciating death on a cross. He also entered into the hard spaces of adversity and suffering of others so that he could provide consolation and healing.

Scripture also asserts that earthly trials and tribulations and suffering are inevitable.9 Ann Voskamp echoes this theme when she writes in her book, *The Broken Way, a daring path into the abundant life,* "this is the deal we all get: guaranteed suffering. We all get it. It is coming, unstoppable, like time…We are not in control, and we never were."10 She further contends that,

> "…there isn't a barrier in the world that can block out pain. There isn't a wall that you can build that protects you from pain. Addiction, escapism, materialism, anger, indifference – none of these can stop pain – and each one creates a pain all of their own. *There is no way to avoid pain. There is no way to avoid brokenness. There is absolutely no way but a broken way.*"11

Yet, when these realities around suffering are ignored or avoided or repressed or kept at a cognitive level, they cannot become embedded and internalized at a deep, heart level. As a result, when misfortune strikes, as it surely will, we are caught off guard.

There are likely many reasons that the church and individuals try to avoid adversity and entering into suffering experiences. Perhaps one reason is that loss and suffering are intense and emotionally demanding. It can be exhausting to even think about entering into someone else's grief and help carry their sorrow in addition to our sorrows. And whenever others experience major losses such as death, it can intensify our fears of losing loved ones or of our own mortality.

I think our western secular culture tends to focus on the pursuit of happiness, achieving prosperity and becoming successful. As they chase after happiness and security, they will do everything they can to avoid suffering and to deny death.

I have also wondered about the degree to which social media and the media have influenced the way we view and deal with suffering. On social media platforms there can be such a false sense of positivity where life is good, and we are doing great that it doesn't capture or reflect the hard truths of what is actually going on in people's lives. And every day, we are exposed to multiple stories and graphic images from around the world that depict human adversity. Yet, we cannot possibly respond to every single situation. Over time, in order to cope we grow immune to the adversity we witness and we minimize our responsibility to help and offer consolation to others.

Brené Brown adds to this discussion when she suggests that part of this avoidance stems from the human preference to feel more positive emotions such as amusement, pleasure or contentment. She discusses this in her book, *Rising Strong*, when she writes,

> "We don't like how difficult emotions feel, and we're worried about what people might think. We don't know what to do with discomfort and vulnerability. Emotion can feel terrible, even physically overwhelming. We can feel exposed, at risk, and uncertain in the midst of emotion. Our instinct is to run from pain. In fact, most of us were never taught how to hold discomfort, sit with it, communicate it, only how to discharge or dump it, or to pretend that it's not happening. If you combine that with the instinctual avoidance of pain, it's easy to understand why off-loading becomes a habit. Both nature and nurture lead us to off-load emotion and discomfort, often onto other people."[12]

I have also wondered the degree to which our culture that prioritizes goal setting, multi-tasking, working hard, and finding swift solutions, prevents people from sitting in the spaces of suffering and embracing discomfort. The well-known saying, "Just do it," reflects the ideal that anyone can do anything, just by setting goals and working hard enough. While I do believe in the efficacy of goal setting and positive thinking in helping us to achieve our goals and to prosper, I also believe it is equally true that there are no guarantees that life will unfold the way we want. Unforeseen circumstances will often interrupt our plans. Hardship will arrive at our front door, harrowing phone calls will awaken us in the middle of the night, or a trusted friend will turn on us without warning.

I learned this the hard way. As a young girl, my father instilled the notion of positive thinking, teaching my siblings and me that if we put our minds to something and worked hard, it was possible to achieve anything. And for the most part, this notion had proven to be a worthy strategy in helping me achieve my goals. So, when I set goals in high school to make the Canadian National Track team and represent Canada at the Olympic Games, I was very confident I could make it happen. And as planned, I was selected to the Canadian National Track Team right after I graduated from high school. Then after six years of running for Canada and medaling in several major competitions such as the Commonwealth Games, Pan American Games, Pan Pacific Games and two World Cups, my sights were set on making the 1980 Canadian Olympic Team. I was euphoric when I won the 800 meters at the Olympic Trials and was selected to run the 800 and the 4 x 400 relay at the Olympic Games.

The Canadian athletes' flights were booked to Moscow. My Olympic uniform and tracksuit had arrived in the mail. My husband, parents and siblings were all flying to Moscow to watch my races. My training had been going extremely well and I was ready to compete. But then just a few weeks before the Canadian team was scheduled to leave for the Games, I was lingering over my breakfast and I happened to glance at the daily newspaper. I was blindsided by the headlines. Canada was joining the United States in boycotting the Olympic Games due to their objection over Russia's invasion of Afghanistan. It is the only time that Canada has ever boycotted the Olympic Games and prevented their Canadian athletes from competing. So, even though I officially remain an Olympian and I am a member of the Canadian Olympic Association, the unexpected boycott denied the entire Canadian Team and me the opportunity to actually compete in the Olympics.

Wrestling with such a major loss was the first time I faced the reality that sometimes, no matter how good we are or how hard we work, we cannot guarantee the outcomes we desire. Life is unpredictable, and unforeseen events can force us to walk through seasons of unexpected, unwarranted loss and grief. My example highlights the high value we can all place on goal setting, personal control, power, accomplishments, and earning prosperity. And whenever something illuminates that we are not in ultimate control over how life unfolds, we are compelled to consider the Someone who is.

I believe that when the church body becomes more willing to move into authentic reflection and functional conversations about suffering, spaces will be opened for healthy discussion around loss and grief. This discussion will build a more robust theology and methodology of suffering and cultivate the capacity for people to become more engaging, affirming, and compassionate when grief descends.

I believe that the Book of Job is one resource that can help us to achieve these goals. As Ellen Davis contends, the Book of Job is "immeasurably more than a theology of suffering. It [also] gives us the theology of a sufferer."[13] Job's narrative invites us to enter into his suffering narrative, where we witness his struggle to understand his loss and grief, God's role in suffering, and how to provide consolation. His narrative permits us to learn through his experiences.

As we first enter into Job's narrative, we find ourselves sitting in the ashes alongside Job on the garbage heap, just outside the city gates. We then witness his companions' arrival, their initial grieving, wailing, ripping their robes, and throwing dust on their heads. Then they lapse into silence and sit quietly with Job for seven days. We get to listen in as they begin to speak and wrestle with understanding *why* Job is experiencing such misfortune, where God's justice is, and how Job might be able to regain his prosperity.

As we eavesdrop on their often-heated conversations, it is disconcerting to overhear the companions' misguided attempts to console him. Yet, the companions' heartless behavior and speech can provide helpful insights about how to move from being miserable comforters into being consoling comforters.

In the epilogue, Job, his companions, and the reader never get answers about why Job's life was interrupted and why he had to suffer while others seemed to prosper. However, God's speeches do provide them (and the readers) a glimpse of God's character, his sovereignty, and his utter delight in creating and managing every single thing he has created. Robert Alter in, *The Art of Biblical Poetry,* suggests that God's speeches take Job and the reader,

> "...beyond [our] human plight [into an] immense world of power and beauty and awesome warring forces. This world is permeated with God's ordering concern, but as the vividness of the verse makes clear, it presents to the human eye a welter of contradictions, dizzying variety, energies and entities that man cannot take in. Job surely does not have the sort of answer he expected, but he has a strong answer of another kind."[14]

Ultimately, I pray that this book and its focus on what the Book of Job can teach us about suffering will stimulate thoughtful reflection and fruitful discussions. I pray by the book's conclusion it will have achieved three specific integrated goals: First, that readers will have begun to form a Christian theology of suffering; second, that readers will have acquired at least a basic understanding of loss and grief; third, that readers will have learned some practical skills that will help them to navigate suffering experiences and become more consoling comforters.

I fully acknowledge that inviting you to wade into the topic of suffering may seem intimidating. But please be reassured because this invitation is actually a paradox. For a while, it is true that loss and grief can be an uncomfortable, emotionally charged topic, it is also true that understanding suffering will build your capacity to be consoling, empower your Christian walk, deepen your relationship with God and others, and better prepare you to navigate suffering.

Due to the parameters of this book, it is only possible to briefly reference how Jesus enters into these Old Testament conversations between Job and his companions. These references relate to how Jesus and some of the New Testament revelations shifted the Old Testament's understanding of God and suffering. I encourage you to join me in a life-long pursuit of forming a robust understanding of suffering and becoming more consoling and compassionate comforters.

Dallas Willard addresses this idea of continual, life-long growth in his book, *The Allure of Gentleness, Defending the Faith in the Manner of Jesus*. He contends that it will be through our ongoing experiences, reading, studying, and discourse we will continue to be transformed. "You see, I don't live with the assumption that I am right about everything, but I do live with the assumption that we should earnestly inquire and use our minds together under God to seek understanding."[15]

So, please join me as we enter into Job's narrative, walk alongside him in his suffering and grief journey, ask the hard questions, learn some skills, and begin to form an understanding of suffering so that we can continue to grow in our capacity to become more consoling comforters when grief descends.

Reflections and Applications:

1. Read or re-read the *Book of Job* in your preferred biblical translation.

2. Read the *Brief Summary of the Book of Job* in Appendix A, which provides an outline summarizing the main points in Job's narrative.

3. Spend some time reflecting and journaling on Brené Brown's, Ellen Davis', Timothy Keller's, Walter Brueggemann's, Nancy Reeves', Leslie C. Allen's, and Ann Voskamp's quotes.

4. Go back through the chapter and take note of the questions. Take the time to discuss and ponder the questions, and to journal about your thoughts. As you do, reflect on one or more of your personal experiences with loss and suffering and how these compare and contrast with Job's and Anne's experiences.

5. Watch the *Bible Project – Book of Job* on YouTube. It is a short, animated video that will help you grasp the Book of Job's basic narrative and its main themes.[16]

Reflection Questions on the Video:

- o What did you learn about Job and his companions' theology of suffering?

- o What did God say to Job and his companions about the way they should walk through suffering?

- o Job and his companions held onto a reward and retribution theology, where the righteous are rewarded with prosperity and blessings, and the wicked are punished with suffering. Reflect on this theology and how it has influenced our understanding of suffering.

o God's speeches in the epilogue reveal his divine character, his utter delight in creating, and in managing all that he creates. How might seeing God in this light influence how we see him in our seasons of prosperity *and* suffering?

o As we witness Job walking through excruciating loss, what are some of your initial thoughts about how suffering transforms us?

o In your experiences of loss and grief, what questions have you personally struggled to find answers for?

Chapter Two
What The Book Of Job Reveals About Suffering

"Then Satan answered the Lord, 'Does Job fear God for nothing? Have you not put a fence around him and his house and all that he has, on every side? You have blessed the work of his hands, and his possessions have increased in the land. But stretch out your hand now, and touch all that he has, and he will curse you to your face" (1:9-11).

"While [the messenger] was still speaking, another came and said, 'Your sons and daughters were eating and drinking wine in their eldest brother's house, and suddenly a great wind came across the desert, struck the four corners of the house, and it fell on the young people, and they are dead; I alone have escaped to tell you.' Then Job arose, tore his rob, shaved his head, and fell on the ground and worshiped. He said, 'Naked I came from my mother's womb, and naked shall I return there; the Lord gave, and the Lord has taken away; blessed be the name of the Lord" (1:18-22).

As we open up the Book of Job and step into the first pages of Job's narrative, we are introduced to two major threads that set the backdrop for the story. The first thread, regarding Job's reasons for being righteous, is woven into a conversation between God and Satan that takes place in heaven.

19

The second thread describes the main figure, Job, an innocent man, and how his prosperity and his sense of God is tested by a series of unfathomable tragedies, including the deaths of his ten children, devastating health issues, the loss of his entire estate, and his status as an esteemed elder in the community.

In the heavenly conversation, Satan questions God about Job's motives for being faithful. He contends that Job is only righteous because of how God has so generously blessed him and allowed him to flourish (1:6-12). Satan further contends that if Job were to experience adversity, he would quickly turn away from God and curse him to his face (2:1-10).

God disagrees. He declares that Job is the most righteous man on earth and believes that Job's faith and reverence are genuine. God is confident that Job will remain faithful and persist in his integrity even if he is forced to experience trials and suffering (2:3).

E. Ray Clendenen writes in his article, *The Message and Purpose of Job,* that "The word integrity, *yashar,* in the Old Testament, refers to something that is straight or level and conforms to a standard. When speaking of a person, it is often translated to mean 'upright,' referring to someone whose way of life conforms to what is right, and who follows the Lord's ways, his ethical and moral standards of behavior."[1] Based on Clendenen's definition, it is clear that God believed Job was a man of integrity because he was sincere about obeying God's will and turning away from evil.[2]

God was so confident in Job's righteousness that he permitted Satan to test Job. But, he did attach a stipulation, "Very well, all that he has is in your power; only spare his life!" (1:12; 2:6).

The reader is privy to this heavenly discussion, but Job never learns about it.

The reader immediately wonders, "Will Job remain faithful when tested?" "What in fact does motivate Job to be righteous?" "Does he lead a righteous life because he loves God, or is it because of what God gives him?"

Perhaps their heavenly discussion also stirs the reader to turn inwards and reflect on their own motivations for being faithful. Reflecting on the degree to which our faith is influenced by the idea that God blesses obedience and punishes disobedience, this prompts us to consider:

o Why does a good God allow good people to go through tests and suffer?

o Are there reasons why we believe that we should be exempt from experiencing adversity?

o Is every trial and hardship a form of testing?

o What might we learn about God's character and power when he permitted Satan to test Job, but put limits on the testing?

o What might God say about our faithfulness and integrity?

o How will we respond when we are tested like Job and have to walk through adversity?

As readers, we are intrigued to discover how Job will respond in his adversity and what his trials will reveal about the state of his heart. But, almost at once, we may predict that the best indicator of the state of Job's heart will not be what he has said and done in his season of prosperity, but rather we sense that the most accurate measure of his heart is going to be revealed in how he will respond in adversity. We saw these ideas played out in the movie, *Titanic,* where all the passengers appearing pleasant and agreeable, as long as the ship was sailing smoothly. Yet, the very moment the ship starts to sink and there is adversity, the true state of the passengers' hearts are exposed. And while there were some passengers who continued to obey directions and cooperate and help others, there were others who were willing to shove people out of the way so they could seize a place in a lifeboat.

Like Job and the Titanic passengers, our winter season exposed the state of my heart and the heart of everyone touched by our trials. Some tried to avoid suffering by withdrawing. Some sought to take care of their own needs at the expense of others. Others were willing to lean into the hard spaces of suffering and help where they could to provide consoling comfort. Sometimes people swung from one extreme to the other, depending on how emotionally stretched they were on any particular day.

In an abstract, intellectual way, I had understood that darkness had entered the world after the Fall in the form of troubles, selfishness, deceit, illness and death.3 But, as I walked through my suffering experiences, these abstract thoughts became concrete, tangible experiences. The truth of our human nature and existence is that we all fall short in choosing truth, integrity and righteousness. This human struggle is more likely to manifest itself whenever we are in the midst of a crisis.

At this point, I think it is important to differentiate that suffering can be either merited or unmerited or a mix of both. When our poor choices lead to harmful outcomes for ourselves and others, it is called *merited suffering*. This is suffering that has been caused by identifiable human wrongdoing or poor choice. Examples of merited suffering are when a chronic gambler suffers bankruptcy, or a driver must relinquish their driving license because of driving under the influence, or an uncooperative, defiant employee is fired for the dissension they have created amongst the staff.

In contrast, *unmerited suffering* is when there is no apparent cause or explanation for the suffering. It is unexpected, unearned and undeserved suffering. Unmerited suffering occurs in situations such as when a child is diagnosed with Crohn's disease, or a partner unexpectedly ends a relationship, or a basement floods due to a natural disaster. Job's suffering was unmerited because the heavenly conversations revealed that Job had done nothing to deserve his adversity. Whenever people are burdened by such unjust tribulation, or they are persecuted because of their faith, it can be referred to as unmerited suffering.4

Whenever adversity is unpredictable and unexpected, it can feel as though God is just being capricious, indifferent or unjust. As we continue to follow Job's narrative, we will observe how he wrestled with this very issue. As Job laments, there are points where he blames God for his suffering and accuses God of wanting to hurt, destroy and torture him for no apparent reason.5 Job was so baffled by his inexplicable suffering that he repeatedly demanded an opportunity to discuss his case with God so that he could find out why he had to face such adversity (13:3; 23:4; 31:35).

As we return to the narrative and the first heavenly conversation has just concluded, Satan sets out to test Job. As Job's ten children were eating and drinking wine in the eldest brother's home, a strong desert wind struck the house, causing it to collapse. All ten children were instantly killed. At the same time, a series of events killed all of his servants and livestock (1:13-19). Even though Job was devastated by these unmerited losses, he remained resolute in his faith and blessed the Lord saying, "Naked I came from my mother's womb, and naked shall I return there; the Lord gave, and the Lord has taken away; blessed be the name of the Lord" (1:21). The narrator also reveals that, "In all of this Job did not sin or charge God with wrongdoing" (1:22).

Satan then returned to the heavenly realm and presented himself to God. When God remarked that Job had remained faithful, Satan was still convinced that Job would abandon his integrity if faced with further adversity. God allowed Satan to continue testing Job (2:6). Once again, Satan left the presence of the Lord and proceeded to test Job with another series of calamities that included the total destruction of his prosperity and covering Job with inflamed sores from the soles of his feet to the crown of his head (2:7). Tremper Longman III writes in his commentary that these sores "were injurious and threatened death."6 These sores were so itchy and painful that Job resorted to scratching them with a broken pot shard he found in the rubbish heap (2:8).

Job's physical ailments added to his long list of losses. Now, he also has lost his health and comfort. But it is also important not to miss how this verse situates Job on a garbage or dung-heap, outside the city gates. In his *World Biblical Commentary, Job 1-20,* David J. A. Clines discusses the significance of this when he writes, "…it is almost universally assumed by interpreters that the ashes in which Job sits are in the public ash heap outside the town, the resort of outcasts and persons with infectious diseases, as well as, in cases like the present, those who psychically identify themselves with the rejected and the destitute."7

When Job's open sores made him unclean, he was forced to leave his community and sit alone outside the city gates. This resulted in Job sustaining even more losses. The moment Job was labelled unclean, he lost his standing within the community. When Job was compelled to leave the community, he lost his social network and the community's support and regard. And finally, when Job lost his prestigious standing and was forced to identify with the outcast, the broken and the rejected, he would have experienced a loss of dignity and a sense of his personal worth.

Being isolated, marginalized and rejected by one's social network in loss and suffering has continued to occur across cultures and time. This isolation can be most manifested when a sufferer is battling ailments such as dementia or cancer or post-traumatic stress disorder. Job's isolation reminds us of how critical it is to maintain regular contact with a sufferer, reaching out to them with compassion and deference so that their dignity is maintained, and they are drawn back into the community and social support.

As we continue to follow the narrative, Job's wife is suddenly introduced (2:9-10). She is never named, and she utters only one line in the whole book, "Do you still persist in your integrity? Curse God, and die" (2:9). Job rebukes her, telling her, "You speak as any foolish woman would speak. Shall we receive the good at the hand of God, and not receive all the bad?" (2:10). The author then repeats, "In all this, Job did not sin with his lips" (2:10).

Roger Scholtz, in his article, "'I Had Heard of you…but Now, My Eye Sees You': Revisioning Job's Wife," discusses how the conventional interpretations of Job's wife and her one comment have been largely unfavorable and she has been criticized and dismissed as being "rather irrelevant to the book as a whole."[8] F. Rachel Magdalene and Daniel Darling both echo Scholtz's comments in their articles that also focus on Job's wife, when they write how she has traditionally been labelled such things as a harpy, shrew, nag and a handmaid or a messenger of Satan.[9] Longman and Clines concur with these comments in their commentaries when they write that she has most commonly been interpreted as lacking compassion and as encouraging Job to curse God and invite his own death.[10]

Despite the fact that traditional scholarship has often marginalized her, some recent scholarship interprets Job's wife and her one statement quite differently. These scholars suggest that the purpose of her comment was not to nag Job, but to challenge him to hold onto his integrity and reconsider his theology. Clines suggests that the wife's comment may be the powerful catalyst that ends up inspiring Job's moral and spiritual development and theological transformation:

> "She had immediately, or (shall we say?) instinctively, seen what Job will take some time to realize, that he cannot both hold fast his integrity and bless God; either Job or God must be guilty. Though Job never does 'curse' God, strictly speaking, his railing, ranting, protesting, and summoning of his divine assailant is nothing like 'blessing' God either. Though he does not follow his wife's advice to the letter, he is from this point onward infused by its spirit."[11]

Ellen van Wolde, in her article, *The Development of Job: Mrs. Job as Catalyst,* contends that it is the wife's single comment that galvanizes Job to reflect on his theology, by "awakening doubt in him. Job is no longer sure of anything and begins to ask himself questions."[12] Carol Newsom et al in their commentary, *The Women's Bible Commentary,* echo van Wolde's thoughts when they contend that,

> "Her question could be understood in two different senses. She could be heard as saying: 'Do you still persist in your integrity (= righteousness)? Look where it has gotten you. Give it up, as God has given up on you. Curse God, and then die.' Or she could be understood as saying: 'Do you still persist in your integrity (= honesty)? If so, stand by it and say what is truly in your heart. Curse God before you die.'"[13]

These scholars argue that because she was Job's wife, she would have been certain that Job was innocent. And because she knew the state of her husband's heart, she would have also understood that God had not lived up to the covenant or bargain in their reward and retribution theology; that his good behavior should be rewarded. This detail is important because, as Newsom et al point out, it changes the context for her comment. The wife's confidence in Job's integrity reminds Job of his innocence, which then begins to influence how he starts to process his grief.

The fact Job knew he was blameless served to intensify his struggle and to accept what his wife had already recognized, "that what is at stake theologically in innocent suffering: the conflict between innocence and integrity, on the one hand, and an affirmation of the goodness of God, on the other."14 In the end, these scholars contend that Job's wife simply wanted Job to recognize he basically had two choices. He could hold onto his reward and retribution theology, which would mean that he had done something to earn his suffering. Or, he could cling to his innocence and rethink his reward and retribution theology.

Some scholars have also noted that this quick exchange between Job and his wife occurred just prior to Job falling silent for seven days. They contend that after hearing his wife's prompt, Job spent the next seven days mourning his losses *and* reflecting upon his wife's comment. This view is supported when the Newsom et al write, "when he finally speaks in chap. 3, his words sound distinctly like those of his wife."15

Drawing from Job's grief reactions and his first comments, there are a few timeless and cross-cultural truths that we can notice— truths that help to enhance our understanding of suffering and how to become consoling comforters. First, we notice how, in the first seven days of Job's grief, he remained silent. He seemed frozen and was unable to find any words. Silence and numbness remain common first reactions in loss experiences. They reflect the shock and disbelief people initially experience when confronted with loss or tragedy. The numbness is a protective mechanism because it helps ensure that the sufferer can gradually adapt to their loss rather than have to immediately face the whole reality and be overwhelmed by its enormity.

However, we also observe that as soon as Job opens his mouth and begins to speak, his laments are often incoherent, erratic, and irrational. This cognitive dissonance and erratic thinking are other typical grief reactions. When sufferers are overwhelmed by grief, they can have trouble concentrating and holding their thoughts. Adversity can also result in the sufferer having many questions. As a result, they can end up babbling, repeating things, and even contradicting themselves. Anticipating this type of grief reaction allows the comforter to listen without judgement or censure, and to patiently accept their ramblings as they struggle to untangle their thoughts and deal with their pain.

Third, when Job's overwhelming emotional pain pours out of the pages, it highlights how major loss triggers an emotional vortex. While it can be daunting for a comforter to witness such depth and breadth of emotion, it is important that the sufferer can find an empathetic and tolerant space. Listening opens up the safe spaces where the sufferer feels free to express and process all that they are feeling and thinking, spaces which validate the sufferer's experiences and emotional reactions. In turn, the more a comforter sits in the spaces of suffering and emotion, the more at ease they will become with intense emotions and grow in their capacity to become consoling comforters.

Finally, if one accepts Newsome et al interpretations of Job's wife and her comment, then her comment highlights how a simple observation invites a sufferer into deeper reflection and to consider things from different perspectives. When an observation is well-intentioned and well-timed, it can encourage the sufferer to look at different ways to view a specific aspect of their circumstance, God's role in their suffering, or how they might navigate their next step.

Reflections and Applications:

1. Reflect on, discuss, and journal about the following questions,

   o What motivates you to be a good person?

   o How have you or how might you respond when you are faced with adversity?

   o Reflect on some of the reasons why our good God allows good people to go through tests and suffer?

   o Reflect on why you think that you or your loved ones should be exempt from adversity?

   o Reflect on whether you believe every trial and hardship is a form of testing?

   o Reflect on what we might learn about God's character and power when he permitted Satan to test Job, but put limits on the testing?

2. Job and his companions held to a reward and retribution theology, where they believed that God rewards the righteous and punishes the wicked. As a result, they struggled to understand why Job, a righteous man, was facing such misfortune. Reflect on whether you have ever been exposed to this reward and retribution theology. Reflect on whether and how this theology has influenced your view of God's character and his justice and how you think about suffering.

3. Reflect on your own experiences with suffering. How have people tended to respond in your adversity? What have you noticed about how the church or people in general have responded to someone walking through adversity? Reflect on whether these responses were helpful and consoling or unhelpful and harmful, and why.

4. Reflect on the concepts of merited and unmerited suffering. How might knowing that suffering can be merited, unmerited, or a combination of both influence how we process our grief or view another's grief? How might this knowledge influence the way we provide support to a sufferer? Is there any bias you hold about merited suffering that might interfere with how you provide comfort to another?

Chapter Three
The Conversations

"For there is hope for a tree, if it is cut down, that it will sprout again, and that its shoots will not cease. Though its roots grow old in the earth, and its stump dies in the ground, yet at the scent of water it will bud and put forth branches like a young plant. But mortals die, and are laid low; humans expire, and where are they?" (14:7-10)

"There is no umpire between us, who might lay his hand on us both...where then is my hope? Who will see my hope?... For I know that my Redeemer lives, and that at the last he will stand upon the earth..." (9:33; 17:15; 19:25)

As Chapter 2 winds to a close, Job's companions are introduced:

"Now when Job's three friends had heard of all these troubles that had come upon him, each of them set out from his home – Eliphaz the Temanite, Bildad the Shuhite, and Zophar the Naamathite. They met together to go and console and comfort him. When they saw him from a distance, they did not recognize him, and they raised their voices and wept aloud; they tore their robes and threw dust in the air upon their heads. They sat with him on the ground seven days and seven nights, and no one spoke a word to him, for they saw that his suffering was very great" (Job 2: 11-13).

We can make several observations from this passage that are relevant to our discussion on suffering. First, when Job's companions heard about Job's troubles, they travelled from different communities to be with him. This behavior would have communicated to Job that at least some of his friends were willing to enter into his suffering. Being physically present and providing companionship are two simple, but profound ways to provide comfort.

Second, it is noteworthy that the companions "met together to go and console and comfort him." This suggests the companions had communicated with one another to coordinate the timing and location to meet before proceeding to support Job. The companions also elected to remain with Job for an unspecified length of time. These two details underline some other timeless truths. Consolation and support can be offered in a variety of ways ranging from a quick drop-in visit right after a loss, to periodic visits over time, to an extended stay, all depending upon what best suits a sufferer's needs. Whenever comforters communicate with one another about the how and when of providing support, it helps to ensure that a manageable and consistent level of companionship is provided.

The companions illustrate how important it is for the comforter to express their grief in culturally appropriate ways. The narrator describes how when they drew close to Job, "They lifted up their voices and wept" and "tore their robes and sprinkled dust on their heads." David Clines, in his commentary, suggests that although some of these expressions of grief were more typically associated with mourning someone's death, they would have non-verbally affirmed their friendship with Job and communicated that they empathized with his intense suffering.[1] While these overt mourning behaviors contrast with how most Westerners typically mourn, their behavior does provide us some important insights. Their behavior emphasizes that comforters can show appropriate forms of empathy and visibly mourn with a sufferer. It also highlights the importance of mourning in ways that align with both the sufferer's culture and their faith. And finally, comforting becomes caring and sensitive when a comforter's responses mirror where the sufferer is currently at in their grieving journey.

The narrator then describes how the comforters "… sat with him on the ground seven days and seven nights, and no one said a word to him, for they saw that his suffering was very great" (2:13). Clines explains that the companions' choice of sitting on the ground with Job, rather than sitting on cushions or stools, is a type of mourning behavior that is referenced throughout Scripture. Clines suggests that the symbolic nature of their posture signifies that they are "with him" and are sympathetic to his plight.2 Clines goes on to suggest that while a seven-day period was a standard length of time to mourn, the friends permitted Job to decide the length of the silence.3 He bases his interpretation on the narrator's phrasing: "they sat seven days … not speaking, for [from their perspective of course] they saw his suffering was very great."4

The companions' behavior draws our attention to more things about providing consolation. It underscores how companionable silence is a sacred gift, one that provides a gentle witness to someone's story of loss and grief. Silence opens the ample spaces where the sufferer can sit in their initial shock, have the time to untangle their feelings and thoughts, and determine their pace for recovery and consider their next steps.

The *Spiritual Care Series* produced by the Health Television Network describes the ministry of silence this way: "Silence is a very concrete, practical, and useful discipline," to be used in spaces that are "so holy that words are inadequate and only silence is worthy of the time and place…It is in this silence that the deepest, most divine love penetrates the individual's life issues."5

While we may think that providing companionable silence is easy, it actually can be very difficult. The truth is, sitting in silence can be very uncomfortable. Silence leaves us alone with our thoughts. We can start worrying about what we should say, how can we help, or whether we will say the right thing. So, rather than sit in silence, we end up filling it with chatter or doing things to help. Yet, these behaviors focus far more on us as the comforter and *our needs*, rather than on the sufferer and being attentive to their needs.

Clines' contention that the companions waited for Job to break the silence draws attention to how being patient invites the sufferer to assume control of how things will unfold. Nurturing an environment where the sufferer has the power to make decisions about their healing journey is important. Empowering a sufferer helps them to hold at least a measure of control in circumstances where they have experienced a loss of control over at least some aspect(s) of their life.

When Job finally breaks the silence and begins to speak, it sets off long conversations with his companions. As we eavesdrop on their conversations, we will notice how Job and his companions wrestled with a broad range of theological topics. Analyzing the full theological range of their conversations is far beyond the scope of this book. However, the following discussion has two primary threads that relate to these theological topics. The first thread focuses on the *content* of their conversations with an eye to seeing how their theology affected the way the companions consoled Job and intensified his grief. The discussion also briefly references how Jesus enters into their conversations and invites a shift in their Old Testament thinking about suffering. These two threads continues our focus on what all of this can teach us about providing consolation.

One of the most noticeable things about the conversations is how they reveal the way people in that time period and in that culture viewed loss and suffering. Their traditional, orthodox theology of suffering was rooted in the belief that because God is just, he judges, and he rewards the righteous and punishes the wicked. Arnold and Beyer state in their commentary that the roots of this theology are found in "a simple doctrine of retribution (often called Deuteronomic theology)" where "faithfulness to the covenant will result in blessings in the future while disobedience will result in curses."6 Because Job, his companions and community held to this theology, they assumed that God had been rewarding Job for his righteousness. Likewise, when he faced adversity, they now assumed God was cursing Job and punishing him for some sin(s) he had committed.

They also believed that obedience, confession and making sacrifices were the primary avenues to ensure and maintain a prosperous life and for Job to return to prosperity (1:5, 11:13-19). So, when Job found himself facing adversity, despite being righteous and having made sacrifices, he was confused about why he was suffering. We see this confusion manifested in Job's inconsistent jumble of lament and praise:

> "God gives me up to the ungodly, and casts me into the hands of the wicked. I was at ease, and he broke me in two; he seized me by the neck and dashed me to pieces; he set me up as his target; his archers surround me. He slashes open my kidneys, and shows no mercy; he pours my gall on the ground." (16:11-13).

> "I shout for help, God, and get nothing, no answer! I stand to face you in protest, and you give me a blank stare!

You've turned into my tormentor – you slap me around, knock me about. You raised me up so I was riding high and then dropped me, and I crashed. I know you're determined to kill me, to put me six feet under" (30:20-23, The Message).

"With God are wisdom and strength; he has counsel and understanding" (12:13).

"See, he will kill me; I have no hope; but I will defend my ways to his face" (13:15).

"He is wise in heart, and mighty in strength…" (9:4)

"He has torn me in his wrath, and hated me; he has gnashed his teeth at me; my adversary sharpens his eyes against me" (16:9).

"Does he not see my ways, and number all my steps?" (31:4)

"Since either way it ends up the same, I can only conclude that God destroys the good right along with the bad. When calamity hits and brings sudden death, he folds his arms, aloof from the despair of the innocent" (9:22-23, The Message).

Such confused, erratic, irrational and discordant forms of thinking all continue to be typical reactions in grief.

As the readers follow the conversations, they soon find themselves sitting on the ash heap alongside Job and his companions, considering what is being debated. When I joined the conversations, I also started to ask the hard questions, build my counterarguments, look for alternatives, analyze the support that they were providing Job, and reflect on how my knowing Jesus was influencing the way I was looking at the issues. Wrestling with the issues helped me to clarify my own thoughts, find flaws in my theology, and then refine my own understanding of suffering.

Even though their conversations became heated and combative, they do highlight the importance of being able to process our experiences. When people have the opportunity to engage in self-reflection and healthy discussion, they can begin to tease out their deep-seated core beliefs. Processing also helps us to unearth any preconceptions, biases, myths, misconceptions, values and partial truths that have unconsciously been woven into our belief systems.

The end product or outcome of this processing is that we are able to get in touch with these basic core beliefs and biases. This is important because these biases or preconceptions will leak out into our behavior or speech one way or another. In his book, *Helping Those Who Hurt: Reaching Out to Your Friends in Need,* H. Norman Wright contends that we all struggle to some degree with biased attitudes, "perhaps towards a person who speaks in a certain tone of voice, a person of a certain ethnic group, someone from the opposite sex, someone who reminds you of a person from your past, and so on."[7] He clarifies that these biases may cause us to reject someone without listening to what they have to say because our personal biases get in the way and affect how well we are able to listen. [8]

Rabbi Stephen B. Roberts builds on these ideas in his book, *Professional Spiritual and Pastoral Care, A Practical Clergy and Chaplain's Handbook,* when he contends that a comforter must be aware of their own theological beliefs, not only because they become more self-aware and secure in their beliefs, but because it will help them to be more accepting of the theology of the people being served, "whether they be Christian, Buddhist, Jewish, Muslim, Sikh, Catholic, Humanist, or Atheist."[9] Roberts further contends that when a comforter is secure in their own belief systems, not only are they are more open to understanding others' theology and belief systems, but they are also more able to help them towards healing through their perspectives.[10]

Self-awareness empowers the comforter to become more mindful about how they might react to a situation or a person and how their perceptions may differ from the sufferer's, even when in similar circumstance. This sensitivity is especially important in comforting situations where the comforter may hold to a different faith or set of core beliefs than that of the sufferer. Or in situations like Job's, when a sufferer is struggling to sort out what they believe and need the space to unknot their muddled and confused thinking.

While Job and his companions knew what they believed about prosperity and suffering, problems arose when they stubbornly held onto that theology, even when they were confronted with the anomaly of Job's unmerited suffering. As their rigid adherence to their theology continued to shape their responses, they grew increasingly belligerent and insensitive. Their determination to fit Job's adversity into their theology made them miserable companions. Their refusal to adapt their thinking to the unique circumstances made them miss four key things. They missed how their beliefs negatively shaped their responses to Job. They missed the invitation to see how Job's adversity could help them identify and tweak a flaw in their theology. They were unable to fully *listen to* what Job was trying to communicate. And finally, they either missed or indifferent to how their misguided efforts were intensifying his grief, rather than providing comfort.

In contrast, we see how the truth of Job's innocence pushed Job to question his theology and preconceptions. He had to either adhere to his theology, accept his companions' assumptions and confess to sins he knew that he had not committed, or he had to question his theology. Job cautiously began to explore the possibility that there might be other ways to interpret his adversity and suffering. Once this door was opened, Job was freed to consider many other theological issues, including God's nature and his justice, how a human could present a case to God, and what happens after death.

Job's lament reveals how desperate he was to present his case to God, the good Judge, so that he could get justice and be restored (23:3-7). But he also wonders how he, a mere mortal, could ever plead his case with a holy and omnipotent God,

> "For he is not a mortal, as I am, that I might answer him, that we should come to trial together. There is no umpire between us, who might lay his hand on us both. If he would take his rod away from me, and not let dread of him terrify me, then I would speak without fear of him, for I know I am not what I am thought to be" (9:32-35).

As a result, Job yearned for an impartial umpire, someone who was qualified to act as an intermediary, skilled enough to testify on his behalf in the heavenly courts and win his exoneration (9:32-33; 16:18-22; 17:3). But once again, we witness Job's erratic thinking as he vacillates between hoping for and then doubting the existence of such an arbitrator. But then, at one point he asserts with confidence,

> "For I know that my Redeemer lives, and that at the last he will stand upon the earth; and after my skin has been thus destroyed, then in my flesh I shall see God, whom I shall see on my side, and my eyes shall behold, and not another. My heart faints within me!" (19:25-27).

In addition to wondering about a mediator, Job wondered about what happened after death. Tremper Longman, in his commentary, *Job*, concludes that "Job has no belief that death [would] lead to a blessed afterlife. No, the grave and oblivion are what one can expect when one dies."11 The Book of Job reveals that at this time and in this culture, it was generally thought people just returned to the dust from which they had initially been formed.12 But Job's comments also show that he imagined that death might lead to Sheol, an afterlife with no hope, eternal nothingness, utter desolation and darkness. He also speculated about whether the dead would ever see God and whether death might bring rest and quiet, freedom from bondage, and be a meeting house for all the living (3:11-13; 19:26; 30:23).

We see two occasions where Job deviated from this pessimistic view of the afterlife, where he wondered whether there might be something more hopeful in the afterlife. The first occasion is when he considered the new growth that sprouted out of a dead tree and he reasoned that if dead trees re-sprouted and their roots do not cease perhaps the same thing might be true for humankind (14:7-9). The second occasion was when Job asserted in confidence that there was a mediator or redeemer who would advocate for him, even after his death (19:23-27).

Job's views of the afterlife were varied and nebulous, characterized by uncertainty, but with perhaps, a glimmer of hope:

> "As the cloud fades and vanishes, so those who go down to Sheol do not come up; they return no more to their houses, nor do their places know them any more" (7:9-10).

> "…and after my skin has been thus destroyed, then in my flesh I shall see God, whom I shall see on my side, and my eyes shall behold, and not another. My heart faints within me!" (19:26–27).

> "Are not the days of my life few? Let me alone, that I might find a little comfort before I go, never to return, to the land of gloom and deep darkness, the land of gloom and chaos, where light is like darkness" (10:20-22).

"You would call, and I would answer you; you would long for the work of your hands" (14:15).

"But mortals die, and are laid low; humans expire, and where are they? As waters fail from a lake, and a river wastes away and dries up, so mortals lie down and do not rise again; until the heavens are no more, they will not awake or be roused out of their sleep" (14:10-12).

"For there is hope for a tree, if it is cut down, that it will sprout again, and that its shoots will not cease. Though its root grows old in the earth, and its stump dies in the ground, yet at the scent of water it will bud and put forth branches like a young plant" (14:7-9).

It is reasonable to assume that Job's uncertainty about the afterlife would have intensified his grief around the deaths of his ten children. I imagine that it must have been haunting for Job to speculate about the afterlife that awaited his children.

These issues about justice, a mediator, the afterlife and why a good God allows good people to suffer remain points of confusion for many people. Most of us prefer to avoid thinking about these issues until we too are faced with a major loss experience. As we witnessed with Job, loss and adversity trigger such questions, and the uncertainty about the answers can complicate one's grief. Perhaps if Job had greater certainty around these issues, he may have found a greater measure of comfort in his grief.

In the epilogue, Job and his companions were provided a glimpse of God. Through his speeches, God demonstrated his sovereignty, omniscience, omnipotence and infinite wisdom. While God never provided specific explanations around his behavior or choices, his delight in creating and his love for every aspect of his creation oozes out of the narrative. His divine authority to create as he pleases and hold the mystery behind his choices plays out in the way he chooses to craft diverse and complicated creatures. An example of this is how he created the ostrich, forming it to forget wisdom, having no share in understanding or the ability to fly, yet having the capacity to spread its wings and outrun the horse and rider (39:18).

But then, Jesus entered the world, and we were able to get more than a glimpse of God. Jesus was God incarnate, and he revealed the face and heart of God to humankind. His ministry and teaching entered into these Old Testament conversations and transformed them. Jesus continues to invite each one of us to consider how his life and teaching refines these Old Testament conversations, and how we might now conceptualize and navigate suffering.

As I joined Job in the struggle to understand why a good God allowed suffering, I was grateful that I have the privilege of knowing Jesus because, as we searched for answers, I knew some things that Job did not. I had the benefit of knowing that God remains steadfast in his love, compassion, justice, mercy and grace in both our merited and unmerited suffering. Jesus's life, death and resurrection also offer the possibility of amazing grace and eternal life, which can bring great comfort when we think about what happens after death. Unfortunately, Job could only speculate about all these things.

Timothy Keller talks about these very things in his book, *Walking with God Through Pain and Suffering,*

> "The book of Job rightly points to human unworthiness and finitude and calls for complete surrender to the sovereignty of God. But taken by itself the call might seem more than a sufferer could bear. Then the New Testament comes filled with an unimaginable comfort for those who are trusting God's sovereignty. The sovereign God himself has come down into this world and

experienced its darkness. He has personally drunk the cup of suffering down to the dregs. . . He knew firsthand rejection and betrayal, poverty and abuse, disappointment and despair, bereavement, torture, and death. And so, he is "able to empathize with our weaknesses" for he 'has been tempted in every way, just as we are – yet without sin' (Heb 4:15)."[13]

Keller's comment points out how Jesus experienced human "Job" moments while he was on earth, moments where Jesus personally suffered rejection, humiliation, mockery, minimization, derision, hunger, loneliness, exhaustion, loss and isolation. Satan tested him in the desert. Peter denied him. Judas betrayed him. Thomas doubted him. His brothers disbelieved him. The disciples deserted him when they fell asleep rather than help him keep vigil in the Garden of Gethsemane. The religious leaders persecuted and tortured him and eventually killed him on a Cross. Of all his followers, only John, Mary and a few other women were resolute and faithful to the end, staying with Jesus until his death on the Cross and his resurrection at the tomb. And then, in his final moments on the Cross, Jesus even had a moment where he felt abandoned by God the Father, as evidenced in his poignant cry, "My God, My God, why has Thou forsaken Me?" (Matt 27:46). Knowing that Jesus is so intimately familiar with human suffering and that he can empathize with our misery can offer a measure of comfort to the sufferer (Heb 4:15).

Gary R. Collins notes in his book, *Christian Counselling, a Comprehensive Guide,* how Jesus also "demonstrated the importance of grieving. Early in his ministry, Jesus preached his Sermon on the Mount and spoke about grieving. 'God blesses those who mourn, for they will be comforted,'" he said. And when Lazarus died, Jesus was deeply moved... and he wept with the mourners. Jesus knew that Lazarus was about to be raised from the dead, but the Lord still grieved" and in the "Garden of Gethsemane, Jesus was 'crushed with grief.'"14 Jesus's open display of emotion conveys at least two things. First, it conveys that God sees expressing emotions as a healthy and normal reaction to loss. Second, it affirms that God is deeply affected by what happens to us. Our sorrows matter to God, and he longs to comfort us in our suffering.

The New Testament also reveals that Jesus acts as the mediator between God and his people.15 To know what Job just dreamed about – that there is an umpire in the heavenly courts who is willing to advocate for us in just and merciful ways – can offer us such hope.

Jesus also enters into the conversations about the afterlife. His defeat of death and resurrection to eternal life affirms a perspective of the afterlife that Job could only dream about. This offers a hopeful vision of immortality and eternal life in paradise.16 The disciple John describes it as being an existence where,

> "They will hunger no more, and thirst no more; the sun
> will not strike them, nor any scorching heat; for the Lamb
> at the center of the throne will be their shepherd, and he
> will guide them to springs of the water of life, and God
> will wipe away every tear from their eyes" (Rev 7:16-17).

A vision of an afterlife where we will be in paradise with God and with the saints who have gone before us, where Love wins, all life is made new and conformed to glory, and where all suffering, "tears, disease, evil injustice, and death are eliminated," is in stark contrast with how Job and his companions envisioned the afterlife.17 This perspective of the afterlife offers relief and hope to anyone who has had to face their own mortality or deal with the death of their beloved.

Jesus and the New Testament offer the possibility of consolation in suffering. This was a solace that Job and his companions were unable to fully access. Jesus continues to enter into our suffering and into the conversations adversity provokes, and we are all invited to discern how we will respond to his invitation.

As we conclude this discussion, we can see how these conversations have illustrated a number of timeless and cross-cultural truths around suffering. First, we see from Job's Old Testament cry that "misery does not come from the earth, nor does trouble sprout from the ground; but humans beings are born to trouble just as sparks fly upward" (5:7), to John's New Testament contention that "in this world you will have trouble" (Jn 16:33), to the suffering that we continue to observe all around us today. Second, becoming aware of our core beliefs, spirituality and beliefs about God, and being sensitive about how those beliefs have the power to influence our responses, ought to help us navigate our own suffering and how to become more discerning and consoling when we attempt to comfort others.

Miserable comforters illuminated how the provision of comfort is not about pushing our viewpoints or giving advice, but rather it is about keeping our focus on the sufferer through listening and observing and offering the safe spaces where the sufferer is empowered to process their grief and work through their muddled reactions.

Safe spaces must be cleared for the sufferer to engage in critical inquiry, examination, analysis and synthesis. The value of these spaces is emphasized in the epilogue when God commends Job's questioning, challenging, and lamenting when he twice declares, "My wrath has kindled against you and against your two friends; for you have not spoken of me what is right, as my servant Job has" (42:7-8).

God continues to invite us into these rich and transformative conversations, with him and with others. It is an earnest, open-ended invitation. One that encourages us to be inquisitive and wonder. Test our beliefs. Grow in self-awareness and form a robust understanding of suffering through the lens of the Christian faith. All which better prepares us to navigate our own suffering and provide sensitive, consoling comfort to others.

Reflection and Applications:

1. Reflect on two or three things that specifically stood out to you in the conversations between Job and his companions. Consider what you thought the companions did that was helpful, what things were unhelpful and what you wish they had done differently.

2. Reflect on your own core beliefs and preconceptions about why loss and suffering happens and what you have believed about grief. How might your beliefs and preconceptions influence the way you navigate your own grief or provide comfort to others?

3. Reflect on what your own experience in the church has been in respect to a spirit of inquiry. Consider whether asking questions and thinking and discussion has or has not been encouraged. Reflect on the value and importance of developing 'thinking' Christians, particularly in relationship to the topic of suffering.

4. Reflect on what God's speeches in the epilogue revealed to you personally about God's character and the role he plays in our suffering. How might having a sense of God's heart and knowing of his love for all creation influence how we deal with loss and suffering?

5. Reflect on Job's lament. Consider what his lament teaches us about the tension between trusting in God's sovereignty and questioning and challenging God.

6. Reflect on how knowing Jesus and having access to the Bible might influence the way you personally face trials, process your grief, and provide comfort.

Chapter Four
A Framework For Loss And Grief

"Therefore I will not restrain my mouth; I will speak in the anguish of my spirit; I will complain in the bitterness of my soul" (7:11).

"I loathe my life; I would not live forever. Let me alone, for my days are a breath" (7:16).

"I have sewed sackcloth upon my skin, and have laid my strength in the dust. My face is red with weeping, and deep darkness is on my eyelids..." (16:15-16).

In the prologue, Job exemplified compassion and love in action when he stepped into the suffering of others, rescued the poor who cried for help and the fatherless who had none to assist them (29:12). He wept for the troubled, helped the dying and grieved for the widowed. Later in the narrative, when Job laments how he has fallen from prosperity, he reminisces about how he delivered the poor who cried, and the orphan who had no helper... caused the widow's heart to sing for joy...put on righteousness, and it clothed him; his justice was like a robe and a turban. He was eyes to the blind, and feet to the lame. He was father to the needy and he championed the cause of the stranger (29:12-16).

Jesus also showed tremendous compassion for the vulnerable, excluded, marginalized, poor, weak, disenfranchised and hurting. He turned into the suffering spaces. He touched the lepers, the blind who could not see, the deaf who could not hear. He raised people from death to life. He came to redeem the lost. Jesus lived out God's greatest commandment to love God, love your neighbor and love yourself (Lk 10:27; Matt 22:35-40). During his ministry, Jesus extended a timeless invitation for all people to exemplify this love and to offer consolation (Jn 13:34-35).

The church continues to echo Jesus's call to love others and console those who are hurting. Yet, because the western world as a whole has experienced a greater degree of prosperity, safety, personal freedoms, and a better standard of health care in comparison to many places in the world, they tend to have more limited experience with hardship and suffering. So, when confronted with loss and grief, they are often bewildered about how to grieve and provide consolation. Ultimately, many will try to avoid suffering and leave the consolation to others. And, as we witnessed in Job's narrative, even when people are well-intentioned and decide to help, their efforts can be so misguided and insensitive they cause further distress, rather than consolation. They become like the "miserable comforters" and the "worthless physicians" (13:4; 16:2).

The overarching goal of this book is to build an understanding of loss and grief through the lens of the Christian faith, so that we can process grief and provide consolation in healthier and more compassionate ways. The previous chapters focused on the importance of discerning our personal beliefs, biases, and theology around suffering. The following chapters focus on integrating this self-awareness with a framework for loss and grief and practical comforting skills. Ideally, this will cultivate a greater confidence about facing loss, entering grief, and providing consolation.

An Introduction to Loss and Grief.

Before entering into suffering, it is important that we have a framework around loss and grief. To begin, Gary R. Collins' in his book, *Christian Counseling, A Comprehensive Guide,* offers an insightful definition of loss and grief:

> "Grief is a normal response to the loss of any significant person, object, or opportunity. It is an experience of deprivation and anxiety that can show itself in one's behavior, emotions, thinking, physiology, interpersonal relationships, and spirituality. Grief is not limited to the loss of a loved one through death. Any loss can bring grief, including divorce, [loss of culture or identity, loss of control or power], retirement from a job, amputation of a limb, the departure of a child to college or a pastor to some other church, moving from a friendly neighborhood (or watching a good neighbor move), losing a home or other valued possession, the death of a pet or plant, loss of a contest or athletic game, health failures, or even the loss of one's youthful appearance, confidence, or enthusiasm. Sometimes, desirable and long-anticipated events – like the move to a better job or graduation from college – can bring grief (mixed with happiness) because valuable memories or relationships are being lost and left behind. Doubts about one's faith, the waning of spiritual vitality or the disillusionment about the actions of a trusted religious leader can all lead to sadness and emptiness that indicate grief. In summary, whenever a part of life is lost or taken away, there can be grief."1

While lengthy, Collins' definition provides a helpful description of loss and grief. When people think about loss, they typically think in terms of major events such as death or a break-up of a relationship. Collins' explanation helps to expand our understanding about what constitutes a loss. When we understand that a loss occurs whenever any part of our life is lost or taken away, we can start identifying the losses we and others experience every single day, but which previously may have gone unnoticed and underacknowledged.

Collins' definition also highlights the differentiation between loss and grief. *Loss* is the term that relates to something that has been taken away, whereas *grief* relates to the multifaceted, conflicting feelings we experience as a result of that loss. Job lost his ten children when they died. What he felt about their loss was tremendous grief.

There can also be an anticipatory aspect to loss and grief. In his article, "That Discomfort You are Feeling is Grief", Scott Berinato writes that "anticipatory grief is that feeling we get about what the future holds when we're uncertain..." where we worry "there is a storm coming. There's something bad out there."[2] He proceeds to write that most loss leads to the additional losses around our sense of the safety and certainty of our future.[3] As a result, we end up grieving imagined or anticipated future losses that, in reality, may never actually occur. Nevertheless, it is important to mention this anticipatory loss and grief because whenever we experience a major loss or many losses, we typically will also experience fear at having to face more loss in the future. As we consider an uncertain future and possible anticipated losses, we grieve. The timeless, cross-cultural truth here is that when we walk through a loss and grief experience, we can also lose our sense of safety, confidence and certainty in the future. And as a result, we also bear the burden of anticipatory grief.

In their book, *All Our Losses All Our Griefs, Resources for Pastoral Care,* Kenneth R. Mitchell and Herbert Anderson contend that, "unless we understand that all losses, even 'minor' ones, give rise to grief, we shall misunderstand [grief's] fundamental nature."4 Job's narrative demonstrates why it is so important that we grasp a more robust description of loss and grief. Job's companions focused on Job's obvious losses, such as the loss of his wealth and estate, and his children's death. But what they missed was he had also suffered many other obscure losses including the loss of his status in the community, the hope of future grandchildren, his social network and his confidence about the future. This would have contributed to many of Job's losses being unseen and unheard and unprocessed.

Mitchell and Anderson distinguish that *grieving* or *mourning* is the "intentional work grief-stricken persons engage in, enabling them to return eventually to a full, satisfying life."5 There is no expectation regarding how long it should take someone to grieve and move past a loss. Factors such as the sufferer's relationship or attachment to what was lost, their own physical health and mental well-being, the stress or pressure they are under, their recent history of loss or the nature of the social support they receive will influence the complexity of their grief and the length of time they will need for grieving.

Loss and grief are universal experiences. Every single one of us will encounter adversity and winter seasons. At first glance, many of our loss experiences will appear similar. Yet, even when two losses look alike, they are usually quite different. There are many factors that can influence what a specific loss means to someone. Therese A. Rando, in her book, *Grief, Dying and Death, Clinical Interventions for Caregivers,* examines how every loss will have its own unique nuances, circumstances, secondary losses, value of attachment, and cultural, economic, social and religious contexts.6

This is why a comforter must refrain from making assumptions about someone else's loss or using their own experiences or expectations to compare losses.

Rando further clarifies that a comforter also needs "to appreciate the idiosyncratic meaning a particular loss has for a given individual in order to understand that person's grief."7 Therefore, a loss will have a particular, subjective meaning attached to it *and* the way a person reacts to that loss will be unique and singular. Appreciating that each loss and grief experience is distinctive will help comforters to become more sensitive about how they interpret a loss and the way they provide comfort. Further, this knowledge should deter the comforter from assuming that they "know exactly how someone feels" just because they have experienced or witnessed something similar.

A good example to illustrate the distinctiveness of loss and grief is when Job lost his role as an elder at the gate. It would be easy to assume that when he lost this role, Job would feel dejection and shame. As the reader follows his narrative and listens to him, this assumption would be verified. Job did experience tremendous grief when he lost his role as an elder. Yet, it is possible that someone else might have responded very differently to the loss of this same role. Some may feel tremendous relief and a sense of liberation from not having to carry the heavy responsibilities, the pressures and the time commitments associated with that role.

Rando also describes how there can be a cumulative quality to loss and grief.8 She suggests that when someone faces a series of losses, they can end up experiencing what is referred to as traumatic and complex grief. We see this happen when Job faced multiple losses and he ended up experiencing intense, debilitating grief. In fact, Job experienced such trauma, there were moments he lamented that only death might bring him release from his suffering.

Sometimes it may seem that a person is overreacting to a loss. But it is important to remember that there can be many other mitigating factors around that loss that can trigger such a response. When someone is in a similar situation to Job and they have accumulated many losses, or perhaps even had just one, recent devastating loss, then the addition of even one more loss can trigger an intense emotional reaction.

Each loss also has associated secondary losses.9 These are the losses that flow out of the initial or major loss. For example, when Job's ten children died, each death was a major loss. But what we might miss if we are not careful are all the secondary losses that were attached to their deaths. These secondary losses could have included Job losing his sense of normalcy, regular routines, vision and purpose for the future, having grandchildren, or engaging in the social activities that had once included his children. Because most of these secondary losses remained unrecognized, it negatively impacted Job's grieving process and the companions' ability to provide him comfort.

Rando also describes how losses can be either physical (*tangible*) or symbolic (*intangible*).10 A tangible loss relates to any loss that has a solid or concrete presence, something that can be touched, seen and measured. In contrast, an intangible loss relates to anything that is abstract, unquantifiable, and is less likely to be seen or measured.

Examples of Job's tangible losses included the loss of his children, estate, wealth, employers, livestock, community and physical health. His intangible losses included his loss of hope, security, sense of justice, reputation, self-esteem, trust, comfort, and his theology and convictions around suffering and prosperity. It is helpful to consider a list of Job's losses and reflect on the degree to which each was specifically acknowledged and mourned. What we would notice is that the tangible losses were more often highlighted while little or no reference was made to his long list of intangible losses.

While we tend to think of grief in terms of emotion, grief is actually far more comprehensive. Grief has many dimensions, including how people respond emotionally, behaviorally, cognitively, physically, spiritually, and socially.11 Job's narrative highlights the importance of acknowledging all that the sufferer has lost and all the dimensions of their grief.

When we carefully study Job's narrative, listen to his lament, and attend to the narrator's descriptive details, we are able to gather a more comprehensive and empathetic understanding of Job's grief. The reader can also become more sensitive to how the companions saw Job's adversity through the lens of their traditional orthodox theology, resulting in their engaging in theological debate and offering advice and solutions, rather than helping him identify and grieve all he had lost.

Questions arise about why the companions stuck to their approach to helping Job when their behavior was so evidently wounding Job and straining their relationship. Perhaps sticking to their theology was more about them than it was about comforting Job. Perhaps it was a way for them to feel safer in Job's suffering, more reassured that such adversity could never happen to them. Or, perhaps they never noticed how they were wounding him. Regardless, their stubbornness resulted in their becoming insensitive, miserable comforters.

Evidence of the companion's rigidity and how it caused them to be inattentive to Job's needs are woven throughout the narrative. Examples of how these dynamics play out include when Eliphaz asserts, "Is it for your piety that he reproves you, and enters into judgement with you? Is not your wickedness great? There is no end to your iniquities," and then lists a series of alleged moral transgressions (22:4-9). Later he directs Job to, "agree with God, and be at peace; in this way good will come to you...If you return to the Almighty, you will be restored, if you remove unrighteousness from your tents..." (22:21, 23). Another example of such heartlessness is when we observe Bildad making a tactless comment that implied Job's children had died because they had sinned (8:4).

Because the companions concentrated on their agenda, holding to their theology and using it to substantiate their arguments, it prevented them from fully seeing or listening to Job and being able to comfort him. In addition, their assertion that Job must have caused his suffering, added at least three other intangible losses to Job's long list. Their behavior diminished Job's integrity and self-worth and removed his right to be listened to.

Studying Job's narrative offers us many timeless and cross-cultural truths. It helps us to understand that loss and grief are unique to each individual. Loss and grief can be complicated and traumatic depending on the severity and history of loss. It can be obvious and tangible, and it can be obscure and intangible. Consoling comfort becomes possible when a comforter is self-aware *and* has a posture that focuses on the sufferer and their needs. Because grief can be very complicated, recovery is most likely to happen when the sufferer has the safe spaces to identify and work through each loss and each grief reaction. Finally, in her article, "Providing a Safe Haven, An Attachment-Informed Approach to Grief Counselling", Marney Thompson contends that the goal of grieving is for the sufferer to move from a "loss orientation to a restoration orientation" ... where the sufferer "can learn to experience and tolerate their feelings of grief, reframe how they think about their loss and their future, and envision a future that includes meaningful relationships and life experiences."12

The Nature of the Grief Process.

Grief is the process of mourning a loss. British Columbia Hospice and Palliative Care discusses the grief process in their training manual, *Module 5, Loss Grief & Bereavement Care:*

> "There are many theories on the process of grief; however, we all go through similar phases, thoughts and feelings. Each loss is different and unique – you may not experience all the phases for each loss, nor will you go through them in the same order or for the same length of time. No two deaths are the same and no two losses are the same. Grief around the death of friends or loved ones or [around the same event] can be similar, but it is different each and every time."13

For many years, the process of grief was viewed as a linear process where it was thought that the sufferer worked through a series of stages. It is important to mention that while these theories are still worth reviewing because they bring valuable insights into the process of grieving, more current views propose that grief is far more complex than these previous models suggest.14 As Angela Morrow describes in her article, "The Four Phases and Tasks of Grief," it is now believed that people move through grief in their own distinctive ways, where some might progress sequentially through these stages, but many more will miss a stage, loop back to a previous stage, and spend longer stretches of time in some stage(s) as compared to others.15 Leslie C. Allen in his book, *A Liturgy of Grief,* contributes to this discussion by describing grief this way, "...there is a widely held view that the process of grief consists of a jumble of responses, disordered emotional debris."16

When we keep these ideas in mind and look at Job's grief, we can see that it was not a linear or orderly progression. Job's thoughts were jumbled, disordered and conflicted, and circled back and around. At one moment, Job spoke with confidence about God's goodness and justice. Then, in the next moment, he lamented with despair and confusion about God's injustice, before looping back to praise God.

However, I do think it is important to introduce a few theories of grief so that a comforter will be able to identify some of the commonly experienced grief phases. One of the first theories of grief, proposed by psychiatrist Elisabeth Kubler-Ross, described five normal stages of grief that include:

- **Denial or disbelief.** The first reaction is the refusal to believe that the loss has occurred. This is a shock response that allows the individual to slowly absorb the reality. "No. This has not happened. It cannot be true that I lost _____." "No, not me." "I just can't believe it."

- **Anger.** Resentment grows. "Why me?" "Why did this have to happen?" "This isn't fair."

- **Bargaining.** We try to change things by making a deal, so that things will return to the way they used to be. "Yes, it happened...but..." "God if you only do _____, I promise to do _____." "If I do _____, then things can go back to being the way they were."

- **Depression.** We begin to accept the loss and say "Yes, this terrible thing has happened, and I am devastated." "I am so filled with sorrow over this loss..." "I just don't know how I am going to manage."

- **Acceptance.** We begin to face the loss with a greater sense of calmness. It now becomes a time of looking back, reflection and starting to look forward. "I have begun to process and accept the loss." "I am now trying to move forward and re-engage in life."[17]

If we examine Job's narrative through the lens of Kubler-Ross's theory, it is clear that Job experienced these stages, but not necessarily in a particular order, weaving back and forth throughout his grief process, times where he was in denial, he experienced anger, he bargained with God in his prayer and lament, felt depressed and became so despairing that he wondered if death might be preferable to the pain. Then in the epilogue, we see that Job finally reached acceptance and he began to re-engage in life.

Another notable theory of loss and grief, proposed by British psychiatrist Colin Murray Parkes and psychologist John Bowlby in 1970, proposed a concept of grieving that involved four stages or phases of grief:

- "**Phase 1: Numbness** – when faced with a loss, the person often feels stunned or numb. Varying degrees of denial or disbelief of the loss are usually present.

- **Phase 2: Yearning and Searching** – the person has a strong urge to find, recover, and reunite with the loved one [or the lost object]. Disbelief, tension, tearfulness, and the tendency to hold onto that which has been lost.

- **Phase 3: Disorganization and Despair** – the person gives up searching for the lost person or item. There is some depression, a lack of hope, and loss of purpose.

- **Phase 4: Reorganization** – the person is able to reduce their feelings of attachment and starts to establish ties to new people and things. There is a gradual return of interests and optimism for the future."18

Once again, when we consider Job's narrative of loss through this theory of loss and grief, we can observe him experiencing all four of these phases. At the beginning of his narrative, we see Job sitting quietly and silently for seven days, in a state of shock and numbness. We also witness Job experiencing a range of feelings, including yearning, disbelief, depression, a loss of hope and a sense of purpose. In the epilogue, Job starts to reorganize his life as he establishes relationships with his ten children, re-establishes ties to his community, and there is a sense that he once again feels optimistic about his future.

Walter Brueggemann offers us another way to view grief. He described grief by using the model that he developed to explain the whole Book of Psalms and how human life moves through the various seasons or circumstances of life. In his book, *Spirituality of the Psalms*, the Old Testament theologian and scholar proposes a model of orientation-disorientation-new orientation to explain the way humans find themselves in one season or circumstance, their movement to another season, and "changing and being changed."19 He suggests that humans can be surprised by, and resistant to the change and movement that unpredictably happens to us. Briefly, Brueggemann's model describes these phases as,

> **Orientation:** These are "seasons" of well-being that evoke gratitude for the constancy of blessing."20 This season or circumstance of life is characterized by contentment for how God has created, organized and managed life, a close relationship with God, trust in his goodness and justice, and praise for his provision and protection. The emotions experienced in this season include joy, delight, contentment, hope, gratitude and trust.21

Disorientation: This season reflects changed circumstances, movement and transition. There is "a dismantling of the old, known world and a relinquishment of safe, reliable confidence in God's creation."22 This is a season of loss and brokenness, disruption and disarray, confusion and pain. In this season, the relationship with God becomes strained when he is questioned and blamed through complaints, laments and petitions. Emotions experienced in this season range from despair, confusion, resentment, disbelief, denial, anger, hostility, shame, guilt, uncertainty, hurt to alienation.23

New-orientation: This season reflects the shift out of disorientation and darkness. When we become "overwhelmed with the new gifts of God, when joy breaks through the despair."24 This is a season where there is newness and growth. The relationship with God has been restored; a deeper understanding of God's sovereignty has been achieved; suffering has been worked through. There is a return to praise for God's provision, restoration and salvation. Emotions experienced in this season include amazement, joy, wonder, thanksgiving, celebration, and awe.25

Of all the possible theories or models to explain the process of grief, Brueggemann's model most resonates with me for a number of reasons. First, while his model includes the idea of stages, it also encapsulates how we shift and move between and through the phases of grief. This acknowledges both the phases and the movement between the phases in the grief process.

His focus on movement and change brilliantly conveys the fluid, dynamic and cyclical nature of grief and the seasons of life. This refocuses the attention away from the idea that grief is a linear or constant progression towards a more accurate perception of how, in reality, grief cycles and loops, ebbs and flows. We intuitively recognize how yesterday's season of orientation has or will shift to disorientation and new-orientation, and then circle or loop back around to orientation.

I also appreciate how Brueggemann's model references the complex interplay between the emotional, behavioral and spiritual grief reactions. This is evidenced when he addresses how a sufferer's thoughts and feelings about God typically shift in the different seasons. It is also demonstrated when he discusses how life and grief are a progression and a process that leads to our spiritual, emotional and cognitive transformation.

Brueggemann's model is probably the best lens with which to view Job's narrative of suffering and how he processes his grief. Perhaps this is because the prologue could be viewed as the orientation phase, the body of the narrative as the disorientation phase, and the epilogue as the new-orientation. Perhaps it is because one of the main themes of Job's narrative is how his suffering season influenced his perceptions of God, how his relationship with God shifted as he processed his grief, and how he was transformed by suffering and grief.

Job's narrative of loss and these current loss and grief theories are mutually illuminating. They help clarify many truths about processing grief and providing comfort. How people grieve and process their grief is individual and unique. Individuals move through grief at their own pace, in their own distinctive ways, for different lengths of time, cycling and looping back and forth through phases they already experienced. Understanding the phases of grief and the movements between them illuminates the importance of creating the safe spaces for each individual to process their grief in the manner and timing that works best for them.

Of course, the narrative does not mention that Job was experiencing these commonly experienced phases of grief. In Job's culture and time, the stages and movements through grief and the importance of working through grief would not have been fully understood or appreciated. In fact, even as recently as my childhood, the process of grieving was not fully understood. Traditionally, it was believed that if one ignored the grief and trauma and did not talk about it, it would gradually disappear. Thankfully, the medical and mental health professions have acknowledged and are continuing to research the complexity of grief and how it can best be processed.

This historically flawed belief about ignoring loss and grief was played out in my family of origin. When my older sister was 16 years old, she was involved in an accident that almost took her life. After being rushed to the hospital in an ambulance, she underwent hours of major surgery to save her life, was hospitalized for weeks and then had a year-long recovery period. The surgeons instructed my parents not to talk to her about the accident, convincing them that over time she would eventually forget about it. So, we never discussed the accident and what had happened to her. As a result, her substantial losses and resultant profound grief were never talked about. We all just moved forward. Then, almost fifty years later, my sister approached my older brother and me to ask us about the accident. She wanted to know more about what exactly had happened, how, when and what we were told about it, and how Mom and Dad had handled it. Much of the information my brother and I shared was completely new to her. She also shared with us what it had been like for her. And some of what she shared was news to me. My sister and I were astonished to learn that when my brother had heard she'd been in an accident, he ran to the street corner where it had taken place. He saw her lying there, the paramedics responding, lifting her into the ambulance.

It had become evident that my sister had been denied the opportunity to fully grieve. And here she was, years later, realizing her need to process how the accident had impacted her life and to grieve all that had been lost. But what also caught us by surprize was the realization that the silence around her accident had prevented the whole family from grieving in healthy ways and discerning the how my sister's brush with death had impacted each family member.

In Job's narrative, their inadequate understanding of loss and grief contributed to the companions also missing the totality of Job's grief experience. As a result, they unintentionally created a silence around much of his loss and grief, which also prevented Job from processing all the dimensions of his suffering. In addition, their incomplete appreciation of the grief process negatively shaped the way they consoled Job. Study the following chart and reflect on how the companions' efforts to console Job.

Companion	Comment:	Scripture Verse:
Eliphaz	"Should the wise answer with windy knowledge, and fill themselves with the east wind? Should they argue in unprofitable talk, or in words with which they can do no good?"	15:2-3
Bilad	"How long will you say these things, and the words of your mouth be a great wind?"	8:2

Zophar	"Should your babble put others to silence, and when you mock, shall no one shame you?"	11:3
Zophar	"You will forget your misery; you will remember it as waters that have passed away."	11:16
Elihu	"Pay heed, Job, listen to me; be silent, and I will speak... Job opens his mouth in empty talk, he multiplies words without knowledge."	33:31; 35:16

The companions stuck to their agenda rather than focus on what was best for Job. Their comments ended up lacking empathy and compassion and sensitivity. They denied Job the space to properly process his grief. And their efforts to console Job became so misguided that they ended up wounding Job and adding to his already massive losses.

Miserable comforters.

Reflections and Applications:

1. Reflect on the three theories explaining loss and grief. Was their one theory or any element of the theories that particularly stood out to you? How might they influence the way you think about the grieving process?

2. In Job's narrative, we witness him experiencing multiple types of loss. Using Gary Collins' description of loss, identify and reflect on all of Job's losses.

3. Reflect on Job's losses and consider which losses the companions did or did not recognize, as evidenced by their comments and the type of support they provided.

4. Reflect on why it is important for us to differentiate between "tangible" and "intangible" losses and to recognize both in the grieving process.

5. Consider Walter Brueggemann's model of orientation-disorientation-new orientation and how it might help explain the prologue, the body of the narrative and the epilogue.

6. How might Job and his companions have responded differently if they'd been more aware of the framework and process of grief? How might this knowledge influence the way you would now comfort someone who is suffering?

7. Are there notions or thoughts or biases that have shifted as you have moved thus far through the book? Are you noticing and paying attention to your thoughts and feelings?

Chapter Five
Basic Grief Reactions

"And now my soul is poured out within me; days of affliction have taken hold of me. The night racks my bones, and the pain that gnaws me takes no rest...and I have become like dust and ashes" (30:16, 19).

"I go about in sunless gloom; I stand up in the assembly and cry for help... My skin turns black and falls from me, and my bones burn with heat. My lyre is turned to mourning, and my pipe to the voice of those who weep" (30:28, 31).

"My relatives and my close friends have failed me; the guests in my house have forgotten me; my serving girls count me as a stranger; I have become an alien in their eyes. I call to my servant, but he gives me no answer; I must myself plead with him. My breath is repulsive to my wife; I am loathsome to my own family. Even young children despise me; when I rise, they talk against me. All my intimate friends abhor me, and those whom I loved have turned against me" (19:14-19).

In order to become a consoling comforter, it is imperative to understand that there are phases and movements of grief but also that there are a range of common *reactions* to grief. This is important because when people think about grief, they primarily tend to associate it with emotions. This contributes to them overlooking other common grief reactions. While it is true that loss triggers a mix of intense feelings, it is also true that loss can trigger behavior, cognitive, social, spiritual and physical reactions.[1]

The ideal outcome of this chapter is that it will foster a greater awareness of the comprehensive, pervasive and complex nature of the human reaction to grief. This is critical because it allows a sufferer or a comforter to remain alert to the possible grief responses in each major area. Then when the sufferer's grief reactions have been identified, it becomes possible to process and provide comfort in each area.

Job's narrative is a perfect example to illustrate the importance of understanding the totality of grief reactions. In the following discussion, we will see how Job's companions primarily focused on the thoughts they had about Job's adversity and how he might return to prosperity. This cognitive focus contributed to their missing Job's grief responses in other areas. This hindered how Job was able to process those reactions and the companions from providing Job comfort in those areas.

As we review each of these grief reactions, we will also consider Job's responses, and how the narrator and the companions and how they responded to Job's grief.

Behavior Grief Reactions.

Behavior is defined as the way we act and how we conduct ourselves. Behavior is our observable, external actions, movements, postures. It is one of the ways a sufferer will express their grief.

Some common behaviors associated with grief can include weeping, having trouble sleeping, withdrawal from regular activities, excessive consumption of alcohol or drugs, putting off decisions, verbally or non-verbally expressing anger and hostility, not eating or overeating, intense busyness or restlessness, refusal to show emotion, cleaning out the deceased's bedroom or office or leaving things exactly as they were before the person died.

A sufferer's behavior reactions are often influenced by their culture, customs and traditions. As we witnessed in Job's narrative, some cultures express grief loudly and publicly. In other cultures, grieving is quite restrained and done in private. Culture and family traditions can also dictate grieving behavior, the length of time someone is expected to mourn, what clothes should be worn during the mourning period or to the funeral, when it is appropriate to return to work, or when they may resume regular activities.

In the Book of Job, we observe some common ancient Middle Eastern mourning customs that influenced Job and his companions' behavioral reactions.

Speaker/Narrator:	Observation/Comment:	Scripture Verse:
Narrator	"Then Job arose, tore his robe, shaved his head…"	1:20
Job	"I have sewed sackcloth upon my skin, and have laid my strength in the dust."	16:15
Narrator	"… they raised their voices and wept aloud, they tore their robes and threw dust in the air upon their heads."	2:12

Narrator	"They sat with him on the ground for seven days and seven nights, and no one spoke a word to him, for they saw his suffering was very great."	2:13

The narrator also describes some individual ways that Job behaved in his grief.

Speaker/Narrator:	Observation/Comment:	Scripture Verse:
Narrator	"Job took a potsherd [broken piece of pottery] with which to scrape himself, and sat amongst the ashes."	2:8
Job	"For my sighing comes like my bread, and my groanings are poured out like water."	3:24
Job	"My appetite refuses to touch them; they are like food that is loathsome to me."	6:7
Job	"Even when I cry out, 'Violence!' I am not answered…"	19:7
Job	"My face is red with weeping,…my eyes pour out tears…"	16:16, 20

Job's behavior reactions illustrate some continuing truths about human behavior in grief. Culture, society, families and religious practices can exert influence on how a sufferer may behave in the grief. In addition, a sufferer will have their own unique behavioral grief responses. As we grieve and provide consolation, being aware of how these influences impact our behavior reactions, will allow us to provide consolation that fits for each circumstance.

For example, when we turn to Job's narrative and look carefully for how he was responding behaviorally to his loss, one example we'd immediately notice is that he was using a broken piece of pottery to scratch his itchy sores. There is no mention of whether the companions noticed this behavior or recognized its significance. However, had they noticed Job's behavior, his using a broken shard from the ash heap to scratch his sores, it would have helped them to grasp the degree to which Job was suffering physically, and enabled them to make an appropriate, empathetic response.

Cognitive Grief Reactions.

Cognitions are our mental processes: our thoughts, beliefs, imaginings, knowledge, perceptions, mental constructs and interpretations.

Cognitive grief reactions are another way we respond to loss. They might include thinking about why the loss occurred, how the loss might have been prevented, recollecting the time before the loss, reflections on their current circumstances, imagining the future, a preoccupation with some aspect of the loss or grief, and thoughts about spirituality, God and theology around suffering. A sufferer's cognitions tend to be muddled and clouded and erratic. They may have difficulty concentrating. They can also fixate or get stuck on one thought and repeat it over and over as they work on unknotting it.

When we study Job's narrative and specifically search for his cognitive reactions to grief, we will discover that Job experienced a wide range of cognitive reactions. They are evidenced every time Job shared his thoughts about where God was in his suffering, where he might find wisdom, why the wicked were prospering when he was suffering, and when he thought about his past prosperity, and his current adversity. They are also reflected in what he thought about the way his companions were speaking to him.

Speaker:	Observation/ Statement:	Scripture Verse:
Job	"When I *think* of it, I am dismayed…"	21:6
Job	"But where shall wisdom be found? And where is the place of understanding?"	28:12
Job	"Listen carefully to my words, and let this be your consolation. Bear with me, and I will speak; then after I have spoken, mock on."	21:2-3
Job	"If it is not so, who will	24:25

	"prove me a liar, and show that there is nothing in what I say?"	
Job	"But I have understanding as well as you; I am not inferior to you. Who does not know such things as these?"	12:3
Job	"Why is light given to one in misery, and life to the bitter in soul…Why is light given to one who cannot see the way…"	3:20, 23

It is important to notice that a large percentage of the conversations were focused on processing "why" Job was facing adversity and where God was in Job's suffering. They were preoccupied with trying to find answers, defended their explanations for his suffering, and how they thought Job could return to prosperity.

Because the companions were absorbed with their cognitive reactions to Job's adversity, they denied Job the space to fully express, explore and process all of his scrambled cognitive reactions. Their behavior dismissed and trivialized Job's cognitive responses.

Speaker:	Comment:	Scripture Verse:
Elihu	"It is not the old that are wise, nor the aged that understand what is right.	32:9-10

	Therefore I say, 'Listen to me; let me also declare my opinion.'"	
Eliphaz	"What do you know that we do not know? What do you understand that is not clear to us?"	15:9
Elihu	"Job speaks without knowledge, his words are without insight."	34:35
Bildad	"How long will you hunt for words? Consider, and then we shall speak. Why are we counted as cattle? Why are we stupid in your sight?"	18:2-3
Zophar	"Pay attention! My thoughts urge me to answer, because of the agitation within me."	20:2

These examples help us to draw a few ageless truths about cognitive reactions in grief. When someone faces a loss, they will experience cognitive grief reactions. They think about the loss and ask questions to make sense of what has happened. The questions that most often arise in grief revolve around the "why" of a loss. "Why has this happened?" "Why would a good God allow me to suffer?" "Why am I suffering when others have done far worse?" These "why" questions challenge our belief systems—the way we think the world should work and the way we perceive God.

A comforter's personal beliefs and agenda will shape the ways that they respond and provide support. This, in turn, influences the way a sufferer is allowed to grieve. When a comforter focuses on only one or two categories of grief reactions, it can deny the sufferer the opportunity to work through their other reactions.

A sufferer's cognitions can be erratic, inconsistent, and jumbled. Repeating a thought is also a typical and necessary part of the grief process. Repetition allows a sufferer to hold onto a thought, examine it from different angles, weigh the interpretations, revise the idea, and finally, draw a conclusion.

A sufferer's confused and repetitive thinking can make it quite challenging for a comforter to follow and grasp what a sufferer is trying to communicate. But when the comforter remains patient and quiet, it allows the sufferer the space and time to gradually untangle their muddled thinking.

Emotional Grief Reactions.

Another grief reaction is how we respond emotionally to loss. Emotional reactions include all the diverse and intense feelings that arise when we have lost something. The mix of emotions commonly experienced in grief can include disbelief, numbness, guilt, anger, relief, sadness, bitterness, doubt, emptiness, confusion, peace, frustration, irritability, regret and loneliness.

While Appendix B contains a long list of these feeling words, it only captures a fraction of all the possible words that can help us to identify or label our emotions. The list has been included for a number of reasons. First, it helps to convey the vast number of words that are available for us to use to pinpoint and describe exactly what we are feeling. Scanning the list will also emphasize how few of these feeling words most people actually use. People typically tend to use only a handful of words and often defer to using catch-all type words like "upset," "good," "cool" or "ticked" to describe how they are feeling. The problem with relying on such general feeling descriptors is these words do not capture the full nuance or intensity of an emotion.

To help a client build a more robust feeling vocabulary, counsellors will frequently suggest that a client either post a copy of the feeling words list on their fridge or carry it in their wallet. This allows them to reference it when they have a feeling but are unable to precisely identify it. Referring to the list can help them find the appropriate word to label and communicate what it is they are feeling. Over time, this practice helps them to become more self-aware around their emotions, grow in their capacity to clearly label and discuss what they are feeling, and gradually build a more healthier feeling vocabulary.

Appendix C has a chart of faces, each which depicts a feeling. These types of charts are used in counselling young children as a way to help them find words to describe what they are feeling and learn about and express their emotions. Building a child's feeling vocabulary helps them to better communicate and manage their feelings. I used this chart both in my counselling practice with young children and with my own three children. When our boys were young toddlers, I posted it on our fridge so that we could easily refer to it and start building expressive feeling vocabularies from a very early age. I think posting it on the fridge also helped to legitimize their feelings and their right to express them in healthy ways.

I have also included a feeling faces chart and the titles of two books in Appendix C because they may be particularly helpful for comforters when they are supporting a child who is suffering. Nancy Reeves aptly reminds us that,

> "... as adults do, children need their losses and grief named, acknowledged, and legitimized. Children want to understand death and other types of loss. They learn styles

of grieving – what are acceptable feelings and behaviors – from the significant adults in their lives. And they want to be included in the family's experience of loss, both as grievers and as helpers."2

It is important to also mention that the intensity of any emotion can vary from mild to extreme. A number of factors, such as the person's level of attachment to that person, their loss history or how they interpret that situation, will determine the intensity of their emotional response.

We often assume that we only experience one or two emotions at a time. Yet, in suffering or trauma, our emotional responses can be numerous, diverse, and multi-layered. An image included in Appendix D visually captures how a sufferer's feelings can be all mixed up like a tangled ball of wool.

While grief is most often associated with emotional reactions, the unfortunate reality is that most people have only a minimal understanding of emotions and how to deal with them in healthy, transformative ways. Of course, this becomes particularly problematic in suffering when our emotions are amplified and complicated and scrambled.

As we examine Job's narrative and search for his emotional reactions, we quickly discern the wide range of intense emotions Job experienced. He has an excellent feeling vocabulary, which he used to label and communicate his feelings.

Speaker:	Comment:	Scripture Verse:
Job	"I am not at ease, nor am I quiet…"	3:26

Job	"...I will speak in the anguish of my spirit; I will complain in the bitterness of my soul."	7:11
Job	"I become afraid of all my suffering..."	9:28
Job	"When I think of it I am dismayed..."	21:6
Job	"...Why should I not be impatient?"	21:4
Job	"O that my vexation were weighed..."	6:2

The narrator also reveals to the reader how feelings can be communicated through our non-verbal behavior. We see this in how the narrator takes note of and describes Job's behavior. When he explains the *way* that Job acted or emphasizes *how* he spoke, we observe Job's feelings leaking out of him. Some examples of Job's non-verbal behaviors are when the narrator describes how Job tore his gown, shaved his head and fell to the ground. These behaviors communicated that Job was feeling anguish, devastation and distress. Another way that the narrator communicated Job's feeling was through his use of exclamation marks. Whenever an exclamation mark was attached to what Job was saying, it communicated that Job was speaking with greater volume or intensity. This is important to note because the volume, tone and speed of our speech helps reveal what we are feeling and the intensity of those feelings.

Yet, despite Job's verbally and non-verbally expressing a diverse mix and intensity of emotional reactions, they were left unexplored. First, the companions largely ignored or were dismissive about the way Job was responding emotionally to his losses. Instead, they focused on the cognitive and spiritual issues that were raised, which drew the conversations in those directions. Second, because they were determined to express their opinions and gave long speeches, Job was denied the opportunity to work through his feelings. Third, when the companions ridiculed Job's reactions, he ended up feeling demeaned and belittled. As a result, Job did not have opportunities to untangle, distinguish and process each of his emotional reactions.

The companions' avoidance of Job's feelings had at least something to do with how confused and confounded they were by Job's calamity and what it might mean for their lives and their theology. Feeling threatened by his calamity, they became afraid (6: 21). In his book, *Christian Caregiving, Insights from the Book of Job*, Dr. William E. Hulme concurs with this point when he writes that it "takes self-knowledge and courage" to enter into suffering and it is clear that the "three comforter-counselors were offended by Job's expression of despair and were unwilling or unable to enter into the depth of his feelings."[3]

Most of us lack self-awareness around our feelings. And we are largely uninformed about the range of our emotional reactions in grief and how essential it is to process them. Based on their behavior and speech the companions were no different. This hampered the companions' ability to console Job, just as it hampers our capacity to provide consolation today. When the companions' ignored Job's and their own emotional reactions, it allowed them to focus on what they were thinking, an area where they likely found a greater degree of certainty and comfort.

Speaker:	Comment:	Scripture Verse:

Zophar	"If you direct your heart rightly, you will stretch out your hands toward him."	11:13
Zophar	"You will forget your misery; you will remember it as waters that have passed away."	11:16
Eliphaz	"Why does your heart carry you away, and why do your eyes flash…"	15:12
Eliphaz	"But now it has come to you, and you are impatient; it touches and you are dismayed."	4:5
Bildad	"You who tear yourself in your anger…"	18:4

Their responses unleashed such unsafe relational dynamics, they caused Job to experience additional distress rather than comfort. In desperation, Job begged them to stop.

Speaker:	Comments:	Scripture Verse:
Job	"Have pity on me, have pity on me, O you my friends…"	19:21
Job	"As for you, you whitewash with lies; all of you are worthless physicians. If you would only keep silent, that would be your wisdom!"	13:4-5
Job	"How long will you torment me, and break me in pieces with words? These ten times you have cast reproach upon me; are you not ashamed to wrong	19:2-3

	me?"	
Job	"Do you think that you can reprove words, as if the speech of the desperate were wind?"	6:26

In *The Ministry of Listening: Team Visiting in Hospital and Home,* Donald Peel specifically discusses verse 6:25 when he writes, "Job asserts that words of a sick and upset man must not be taken too literally. He pleads with his 'comforters' to pay less attention to the way he expresses himself and more to the pain and anguish which suffuse his words."[4]

David Clines echoes Peel's observations when he writes in his commentary, "…but here we are invited to view the man Job in the violence of his grief. Unless we encounter this man with these feelings, we have no right to listen in on the debates that follow; with this speech before us we cannot overintellectualize the book but must always be reading it as the drama of a human soul."[5]

In his article, "Mourning, New Studies Affirm its Benefits," Daniel Goleman discusses how recent studies investigating the reduction of grief have affirmed how critical it is for sufferers to have the opportunity to work through both thoughts *and* feelings so that they find healing.[6] These studies also substantiated that the mere act of acknowledging a sufferer's feelings validates them and gives the sufferer permission to explore what they are feeling.

We often blame or give credit to an event or person for making us feel a particular way. We make a direct link between something that occurred and what we felt. We see this evidenced in examples such as, "He made me so angry!" "When she criticized me, she made me feel so inadequate." "When I found out she was talking about me behind my back, I was devastated." Or, "When my boss told me that I had done an excellent job, I was so happy!" When we do this, we are giving credit or the responsibility to some external circumstance for making us feel the way we do.

In adversity, this can become even more noticeable. As the sufferer looks for reasons to explain their adversity, they can end up blaming God for what has happened to them and for how they are feeling. We see this happen throughout Job's narrative when Job accuses God for taking away his prosperity and for making him feel certain emotions. Two examples of this are when Job lamented, "God has made my heart faint..." (23:16) and "...then you scare me with dreams and terrify me with visions" (7:14).

Yet, it is critical to understand that it is not the external circumstance or person that causes our emotional reaction. In reality, it has more to do with what we *think* about that event that causes our feelings.

Jill Anderson, in her book, *Thinking Changing and Rearranging, Improving Self-Esteem In Young People,* uses the following flow chart to point out an essential, but often missed connection between the event and our emotional reactions:

A	B	C
Event/Loss	**Cognitive Reaction**	**Emotional Reaction**
What Happened	What we think about what happened	The feelings that result from our thoughts.7

Anderson's chart highlights that something happens between the event or loss (A) and our emotional responses (C). These are the thoughts we have about the event and what happened (B). And it is these cognitions, our thoughts, that determine or influence what we end up feeling.

A good example to illustrate the importance of this idea is the loss of a parent. When a parent dies, we often assume their children will all experience the loss in a similar way. Yet, even when three children lose their parent (A) we cannot assume all will experience the exact same emotional reaction to that loss (C). When each child has their own unique relationship, history, experiences, and memories with that parent, it means that each will also have their own unique thoughts about their parent's death (B). What they think about their parent's death will contribute to each of them having their own unique emotional reactions (C).

For example, the child who had a close relationship with that parent would most likely think about how much they will miss them, recollect positive memories and remember what they most appreciated about them (B). As a result of these positive thoughts, this child would experience a range of emotions that could include sorrow, yearning, loneliness, and appreciation (C).

In contrast, the child who had a difficult or estranged relationship with that parent would be more likely to think about their arguments, the reasons why their relationship was rocky, and the ways it could have been an easier or a more loving relationship (B). This child would likely experience feelings of regret, anger, resentment, guilt and sadness (C).

Finally, for the child who had been a long-time caregiver for that parent, their passing (A) may lead to thoughts of how they are now freed from the heavy responsibilities of caregiving and how the parent is no longer suffering (B). This child would likely experience feelings such as relief, liberation, hope and anticipation (C).

These connections are very important to understand because, as Anderson points out, they affirm that "not everyone feels the same way when A (an event) happens," even when the event or loss appears to be very similar. 8 "Two different people may have two different sets of feelings. Five people may have five different feelings!"9

Therefore, a comforter should never assume that they *know* how another person is thinking or feeling about a loss. This is true even when the sufferer's loss appears to be very similar to a loss the comforter has experienced or previously witnessed. This emphasizes how important it is for a comforter to remain patient, to listen carefully, and to observe their non-verbal behavior, so that they can draw some impressions about how the sufferer might be responding and feeling.

Paul David Tripp in his book, *Instruments in the Redeemer's Hands, People in Need of Change Helping People in Need of Change,* affirms the importance of being patient and listening to learn when he writes,

> "If you understand the story of redemption, you know that God does not seem to be in the fearful hurry that often drives our efforts to help others. Following his examples means that we can take the time to ask, listen, think, interpret and pray...We do all this to bring the transforming grace of Christ to people as they really are in the midst of what they are really facing."10

Feelings are often described as being either positive or negative, pleasant or unpleasant. In fact, the list of feeling words in Appendix B have been grouped this way. Yet perhaps this is not the most accurate way of grouping emotions because all feelings are valid and, therefore, it is imprecise to describe them as being positive or negative. It is not the feeling that is negative or positive, but rather how we choose to interpret and *express* those feelings. For example, anger is a valid emotion that lets us know that someone or something has hurt, frustrated or annoyed us. It helps us recognize that we need to address and rectify what has so strongly affected us. In this way, anger is a helpful, instructive, protective emotion. But what is problematic about anger is when it is expressed through behaviors like yelling, name-calling, throwing things or hitting someone rather than using respectful words to express what we are feeling and how we would like to see things change.

Paul Tripp adds to this conversation when he aptly points out that God created all our emotions as revealed in how the "Bible paints human emotions with rich and deep colors" and it "captures the full range of human experience and human emotions in a way that only the One who knows the heart could do."[11]

Through Scripture, we see that God created humans to have an incredibly nuanced range of emotions that enhances their enjoyment of the world, but also serve as a way to preserve and protect them. Emotions are a source of information that help humans to make decisions about their circumstances and navigate their worlds. National Geographic's recent publication entitled, *Your Emotions, the Science of How You Feel,* discusses this very idea. One of the articles in the publication, "Distressing Emotions, Fear, Anger, Sadness and Shame," focuses on how these feelings "help us to prioritize what we should pay attention to and prepare to act on. Fear can motivate us to act in self-preservation...Shame lets us know we may have violated a social norm...Anger alerts us we aren't valued and that the relationship might be in jeopardy..."[12]

I often imagine our emotions as being similar to the beeps of a boat's sonar system. In a sonar system, the beeps on the screen alert the captain when the boat is heading into shallow water or near dangerous reefs so that they can then steer the boat away, into safer waters. In our human sonar system, our emotions are the beeps that signal us and relay information to us so that we can also make the appropriate response. For example, feelings such as amusement or contentment signal that we are in affirming and safe environments, whereas feelings such as fear and unease warn us about a potential danger or threat.

Elihu actually references this idea, that pain alerts us to adversity, when he declares, "He delivers the afflicted by their affliction, and opens their ear by adversity" (36:15). In his book, *The Problem of Pain*, C. S. Lewis provides further commentary on this when he writes, "God whispers to us in our pleasures, speaks in our conscience, but shouts in our pain: it is his megaphone to rouse a deaf world."[13]

The intensity of our emotions also relays important information to us. Whenever an emotion rises in intensity, the urgency for us to pay attention to the situation also rises. When fear shifts into terror or horror, these are more persuasive warnings of danger. Or when indifference shifts into attraction, it notifies us that we are interested.

Our current culture seems to favor intellect and rationality over emotion. This emphasis leaves little opportunity for us to learn about our feelings, develop a feeling vocabulary, learn the language of loss and grief and how to manage our emotions in healthy ways. As a result, we often end up feeling uncomfortable when we are confronted by a show of emotion. We are uncertain about how to respond. And when we only possess limited feeling vocabularies, we end up relying on a few, all-encompassing feeling words and miss capturing the extensive and nuanced range of emotions we or others experience.

The minimization of emotional reactions prevents full engagement with our suffering. Emotional signals are dismissed. We can struggle to identify what we are feeling and how to best respond.

And as Goleman contends, our tendency to dismiss or repress emotion hampers how we deal with emotional reactions in grief because it restricts our "ability to deal with the expression of the deep feeling mourning brings."14

The human tendency to minimize the emotional reactions and highlight the cognitive reactions in grief is highlighted throughout Job's narrative. The miserable comforters either ignore or demean Job's emotional reactions because they are so focused on understanding his adversity, and on what they are thinking, that they end up missing the emotional reactions that underlie his words and non-verbal behavior.

Job's lament, questioning, and emotional outbursts obviously distressed his companions. As a result, they struggled to help Job deal with his emotional reactions. Hulme suggests that,

> "...like many of us, Eliphaz was tense and uneasy in the presence of one who experienced great tragedy... Instead of functioning as a physician of the soul, he became a defender of his own view of God and of God's justice in the world. As a physician, one is concerned with the hurt – how it can be cared for and healed. But for Eliphaz, Job's expression of his hurt was a threat to Eliphaz' own interpretation of life." 15

The companions' intellectual and rational responses to Job's suffering prevented them from providing holistic, embodied comfort that would have allowed Job the opportunity to work through the full range of his emotional grief reactions. Oftentimes, comforters still respond this way today. But it is possible to grow in one's competency to deal with emotions. A good place to start is by accepting that God has created humans to experience a whole range of feelings so that we can enjoy life to its fullest. Emotions are signals which help us to understand what is going on around us so that we can more successfully and safely navigate our experiences. Also, whenever someone expands their feeling vocabularies and their language around loss and grief, they grow in their ability to handle the range and intensity of the emotional reactions in grief and provide more consoling comfort.

Social Reactions and Social Consequences

After a loss, people will experience a range of social reactions and social consequences. This is critical to understand in relationship to suffering because as Emily Nagoski and Amelia Nagoski highlight in their book, *Burnout, The Secret to Unlocking the Stress Cycle*, "social connection is a form of nourishment, like food" and "contact with another person is a basic biological need; loneliness is a form of starvation."[16] They discuss how extensive research has proven that,

> "...connection nourishes us in a literal, physiological way, regulating our heart rates and respiration rates, influencing the emotional activation in our brains, shifting our immune response to injuries and wounds, changing our exposure to stressors, and modulating our stress response. We literally sicken and die without connection."[17]

When I recently read these observations in *Burnout*, I immediately thought about Job and his suffering experience. I reflected on how quickly he had been isolated by his community and left to walk through his adversity, largely on his own. From Job's comments and the narrator's observations, it is evident that Job felt rejected, abandoned, and ridiculed by his social network and community.

He was devastated by the loss of their admiration, their companionship, and their support. His lament reveals how these negative social reactions to his adversity ended up becoming some of his most significant losses. His loss of social connection was a loss of soul nourishment; "his loneliness a form of starvation."

When Job was deemed unclean, he withdrew from his community to sit outside the city gates on the ash heap (7:2). This separated him from his social network and the connection they might have provided. Second, we observe that Job's family, friends and community not only isolated him, but they were disrespectful and unkind to him to such an extent he also felt abandoned.

> "He has put my family far from me, and my acquaintances are wholly estranged from me. My relatives and my close friends have failed me; the guests in my house have forgotten me; my serving girls count me as a stranger; I have become an alien in their eyes...My breath is repulsive to my wife; I am loathsome to my own family. Even young childrendespise me; ...and those whom I loved have turned against me" (19:13-15, 17-19).

Social isolation can often be more pronounced when the sufferer is thought to have some responsibility for their adversity and suffering. This heightened degree of social isolation occurs whenever the sufferer's family, community or church distances themselves due to their disappointment, anger, hurt, judgement or sense of betrayal. We notice this happening to Job when his family, acquaintances and his community distances themselves from Job because they believe he has done something to earn his adversity.

Even today, this increased social isolation can occur in merited suffering such as when a sufferer is rejected by colleagues when they lose their job due to alcoholism or the theft of company money, they get lung cancer from smoking and can no longer play golf with their friends, they lose a partner due to their infidelity, or they lose a friendship because of gossiping.

It might be helpful to think of our social networks as systems that are made up of individuals and all the relationships they have with each other. I often envision a social network as being similar to a baby's mobile where the hanging parts represent each individual, and the threads that connect them to the mobile represent their relationships with one another. A mobile or system works best when all the parts are connected and balanced. However, when one of the members is touched by or removed from the mobile through events like death, divorce, moving away, a trauma, or being exiled to the ash heap, it results in significant disruption in the balance and tension of that system. Everything bounces around in response to the change. The system is forced to shift and adapt as it accommodates to that loss. After a time, the system will gradually stop moving as each person and the system as a whole settles down and reconciles itself to what has been lost. This image captures the way Brueggemann includes change and movement as parts of grief.

Adversity can strain even the strongest relationships within a social network. For when even one member in that system is suffering, every other member within that system will be impacted in one way or another. And whenever one of its members leaves the system, either by choice or through death, the remaining members will all experience at least some measure of loss and grief.

Whenever one person is separated or removed from one or more of their social systems (networks composed of family, friends, work colleagues, church groups or neighborhood), it can be a significant stumbling block to their healing. The greater the degree a sufferer is isolated and separated from their networks, the greater the impact it will have on their grief, healing and recovery.

A lasting truth is that a sufferer can end up being isolated from their social networks in their suffering. This can happen when the social network avoids contact with the sufferer and their pain. It can also happen when a sufferer elects to "withdraw from social situations, refuse invitations, have little energy to initiate social contact, and have feelings of isolation, loneliness."18

Job was deeply impacted by the way his community abandoned and isolated him. Once an active, respected and engaged member of his community, their withdrawal and ridicule profoundly wounded him. The loss of his social identity and the absence of their connection, validation and respect, added to his already large constellation of loss.

Finally, it is also important to note that Job felt separated from God. He feared that his adversity meant that God had abandoned him. Of course, his sense of isolation from God, a major form of connection and support for Job, would have impacted him spiritually, emotionally and physically.

Speaker:	Observation/Comment:	Scripture Verse:
Job	"They listened to me, and waited, and kept silence for my counsel…They waited for me as for the rain; they opened their mouths as for the spring rain. I smiled on them when they had no confidence; and the light of my countenance they did not extinguish. I chose their way, and sat as chief, and I lived like a king among his troops, like	29:21, 23-25

	one who comforts mourners."	
Job	"…when I was in my prime, when the friendship of God was upon my tent; when the Almighty was still with me, when my children were around me…"	29:4-5
Job	"I am a laughingstock to my friends…Those at ease have contempt for misfortune…"	12:4-5
Job	"And now they mock me in song; I am a byword to them. They abhor me, they keep aloof from me; they do not hesitate to spit at the sight of me."	30:9-10

Throughout Job's narrative, Job's social support shifted and fluctuated depending upon whether he was prospering or suffering. In the prologue, when Job was enjoying prosperity and good health, he was highly respected and surrounded by a network of family, friends and community systems. He felt connected with God. But when disaster struck, he was rejected by his community and forced to sit alone, outside of the city gate, on the garbage heap. In his suffering season, Job thought God had abandoned him and became distant. And while the companions did provide some measure of social connection in the initial stages of Job's grief, it all dissolved when they began to lecture and disparage him. In the epilogue, we observe that as Job regained his prosperity and was assimilated back into his community they showed sympathy, showered him with gifts, and broke bread with him. (42:10-11).

Living in isolation is in contrast to how God created humans to live within a loving community. God's greatest invitation is for us to love him and all others (Matt 22:37-40). He yearns for his people to live in intimate and mutually caring relationships. In her book *a beautiful disaster, finding hope in the midst of brokenness* Marlena Graves builds on this idea when she writes,

> "It is not good that we should be alone. And God doesn't leave us alone in the wilderness for long. Otherwise, we'd be torn to pieces. He makes available good people—individuals or groups of people who are hospitable spirits—with arms open wide, ready to embrace us and welcome us home with a ring and a robe and a party, people reminiscent of the father in the parable of the prodigal son."[19]

Job's narrative highlights many truths around how we are socially impacted by our grief. First, it illuminates the significance of social grief reactions, highlighting how the presence or the absence of an empathetic and engaged community serves to either help or hinder healing and recovery. Consistent, loving, and compassionate support powerfully communicates to a sufferer that they are unconditionally loved throughout seasons of prosperity and adversity, in both unmerited and merited suffering.

Social connections also communicate to the sufferer that they will not have to walk through adversity alone but will have companionship on their suffering journey. However, the comforter must allow the sufferer to shape the amount or degree of social support that is needed. Sometimes a sufferer will need solitary time, quiet spaces, and the opportunity to reflect and process their grief. Other times, they will prefer the company of one trusted friend, or alternatively, they might welcome a full house with many people and many distractions.

Social systems that remain committed to providing consolation in both merited and unmerited suffering, help to safeguard unity and health within the larger community and church body.

Finally, when God entered into Job's narrative and spoke, he rebuked Job's friends, telling them they had not spoken rightly about him as Job had done. This comment reveals that God had been present and listening the entire time. He had never abandoned Job. Whenever we feel distance from God, Job's narrative invites us to find assurance that just as he did with Job, God will never leave or forsake us, he will always be with us, even when we are sitting on the ash heaps of our lives.

Confused Spiritual Reactions.

Loss and adversity typically cause people to experience a wide range of spiritual reactions.

The Spiritual Care Series quotes John Swinton as defining spirituality as, "meaning, purpose, self-transcending knowledge, significant relationships, love and commitment, as well as a sense of God amongst us."[20]

Collins contends that "even with the current widespread interest in spirituality, many counselling professionals fail to see or admit that there is a spiritual dimension to all human problems."[21] He continues by describing confused spiritual reactions to loss as being the "re-evaluation of one's life, values, goals, and beliefs."[22]

For some believers, their faith and perceptions of God will remain relatively constant throughout adversity. Some will become confused about their faith. Some will reject God in their anger. And for others, such as the skeptic or the seeker, it is often in their adversity where they meet God for the first time.

In Job's grief we witness how he reacted spiritually as he progressed from his certainty about God and his theological beliefs, to questioning God's character and doubting his justice. But after processing his spiritual reactions, and as his questions shifted from "why?" to "who?" Job trusted in God's sovereignty and justice, his theology was refined, and his relationship with God was transformed.

Speaker:	Comment:	Scripture Verse:
Job	"Therefore I will not restrain my mouth, I will speak in the anguish of my spirit; I will complain in the bitterness of my soul."	7:11
Job	"Indeed I know that it is so; but how can a mortal be just before God?"	9:2
Job	"Therefore you say, 'What does God know? Can He judge through the deep darkness?'"	22:13
Job	"Who has put wisdom in the inward parts, or given understanding to the mind?"	38:36
Job	"If mortals die, will they live again?"	14:14

Clines points out in his commentary how Job's speeches expose how "[His] mind is confused, flexible and experimental. In every one of his eleven speeches, he adopts a different posture, psychologically and theologically. In the end, he admits he has nothing to rely upon, not even God—nothing except his conviction of his own innocence."[23]

By the end of the epilogue, Job's dialogue emphasizes that although he had known *about* God, he had not fully known God.

Job now understood that God is incomprehensible, and his ways are unfathomable. Clines further submits that "religiously, Job finds this position acceptable, even actually comforting: to bow in awe before a mysterious God he cannot grasp, perceiving only the 'outskirts of his ways.'"24

Throughout the narrative, Job's companions belittled his spiritual confusion and experimental thinking. They derided Job's thoughts, going as far to call them nonsense and full of air. And to some degree, their comments rang true. Job's thoughts were tangled, erratic and repetitive. But what the companions missed was that Job's verbalization of his unformed, incomplete, and random thoughts was the way for him to untangle, process and make sense of his spiritual reactions.

Speaker:	Comment:	Scripture Verse:
Eliphaz	"Should they argue in unprofitable talk, or in words with which they can do no good? But you are doing away with the fear of God, and hindering mediation before God."	15:3-4
Zophar	"Should your babble put others to silence, and when you mock, shall no one shame you?"	11:3
Bildad	"How long will you say these things, and the words of your mouth be a great wind?"	8:2
Eliphaz	"For your iniquity teaches your mouth, and you choose the tongue of the crafty. Your own mouth condemns you, and not I; your own lips testify against you."	15:5-6
Elihu	"Job opens his mouth in empty talk, he multiples words without	35:16

	knowledge."	

Job's narrative highlights a number of insights around confused spiritual reactions in grief. There can be a wide range of spiritual reactions in grief. Adversity can challenge one's long-standing beliefs about God and his role in adversity. As a result, some sufferers will question their beliefs about God, his character, or why he would allow them to suffer. This happens because the belief systems that had worked so well for them in prosperity may no longer make sense in their suffering. We will also notice that in suffering some will find God and others will reject him. And others will continue to draw comfort and solace from their faith.

Sufferers need safe spaces, characterized by unconditional acceptance and grace, so that they can work through their confused spiritual reactions. To be comforting, we must be open and willing to listening to the sufferer's inevitable questions, doubts and experimental, provocative spiritual ideas. Providing a listening ear and an empathetic heart allows the sufferer the space to grapple with their confusion, find greater clarity and spiritual renewal.

Physical Reactions.

The final category of reactions in grief has to do with how a sufferer is impacted physically in suffering. In his article, "Stuck in the Body," Richard Rohr writes,

> "The body is where we live. It is where we fear, hope and react. It's where we constrict and relax. And what the body most cares about are safety and survival. When something happens to the body that is too much, too fast,

or too soon, it overwhelms the body and can create trauma..."25

Rohr continues, "trauma is the body's protective response to an event—or series of events—that [the body] perceives as potentially dangerous" and "this then gets stuck in the body—and stays stuck there until it is addressed."26

Collins also expounds on these ideas when he writes,

"...bereavement can be bad for one's health because grief can put stress on the body at a time when people are least able to resist the onslaught of illness. Grief interferes with the body's immune system so that viruses and other disease-causing organisms are more difficult to resist especially during the first six months of mourning..."27

Cari Romm, in her article entitled "Understanding How Grief Weakens the Body," builds on Rohr's and Collins' points when she shares that suicide and mortality rates are higher for people who have sustained major loss.28 In her article, she also describes how "English terms for emotional distress are often wrapped up in the language of physical maladies: being heartsick, sick with grief, heartbroken. The Old English word for grief, *heartsarnes*, literally means *soreness of the heart*; *heartache* originates from the Old English *heortece*, originally used to refer to heart disease. The words *hurt* and *pain* can apply equally to the suffering of the mind or of the body. In fact, medical knowledge suggests that our bodies already know what our words have long implied: grief can, quite literally, sicken."29

Typical physical reactions in grief can include:

o   tightness in throat and chest

- o breathlessness

- o pain and discomfort

- o irregular heartbeat

- o a hollow feeling

- o diarrhea/constipation

- o muscle weakness

- o lack of energy/fatigue

- o sexual disturbances/disruption in sexual interest

- o numbness

- o oversensitivity to noise

- o dizziness

- o rashes

- o crying

- o sleep disturbances

- o appetite changes

- o weight loss/gain

- o weariness

- o no desire to eat, food is tasteless

- o chest/stomach discomfort

- o physical reactions also include secondary infections or illnesses such as rashes, colds, shingles, flare-ups of any auto-immune conditions or other chronic health issues. [30]

Throughout Job's narrative, we observe him experiencing many of these physical reactions to suffering.

Speaker:	Comments:	Scripture Verse:
Job	"My flesh is clothed with worms and dirt; my skin hardens, then breaks out again."	7:5
Job	"My breath is repulsive to my wife...My bones cling to my skin and to my flesh..."	19:17, 20
Job	"And he has shriveled me up, which is a witness against me; my leanness has risen up against me, and it testifies to my face."	16:8
Job	"My eye has grown dim from grief, and all my members are like a shadow."	17:7
Job	"The night racks my bones, and the pain that gnaws me takes no rest."	30:17

Yet, even when Job's companions first saw him from afar and noticed the obvious deterioration in his health, they made no reference to the condition of his health. Further, throughout the narrative, there is no mention of whether the companions or Job's community attempted to provide Job any relief in regard to his physical discomfort.

Job's narrative illuminates many enduring truths about physical grief reactions. It highlights how the human mind and heart and body and soul are inextricably linked. Whenever someone experiences significant grief or trauma, their physical well-being will be compromised. Research has verified that the impact of loss on the human body can be so significant that it can make a sufferer more vulnerable to physical illness and other diseases.

In adversity, ill-health and being unable to engage in regular activities creates more loss. This, in turn, can amplify loss and further intensify the emotional reactions of despair and depression.

As a result, comforters ought to be sensitive to how loss can take a toll on the sufferer's physical health. Gentle comments regarding a sufferer's physical state is a simple way to acknowledge and affirm that their physical distress has been noticed.

Soothing someone in the area of physical reactions may be as simple as providing a blanket, a warm sweater, cooking them a meal, taking them for a walk, offering them a cup of tea, helping them shower, offering cool compresses, encouraging them to go to the doctor or providing them space to talk about their physical reactions.

Reflections and Applications.

1. Reflect on behavior reactions in suffering. Consider how noticing and responding to someone's behavior reactions in grief might provide more consoling comfort and improve the sufferer's recovery.

2. Reflect on the role of cognitions in suffering. How might knowing about cognitive reactions in grief influence how we walk through our own suffering or provide comfort to a sufferer?

3. Reflect on the role of emotional reactions in suffering. What stood out to you in the discussion on emotions? How might the discussion on the emotional reactions influence how we walk through grief and provide consolation?

4. Reflect on how Job's social systems behaved and how this impacted Job in his grief. How did Job's social systems help or hinder his grieving process? Reflect what this reveals about providing support to a sufferer in the area of social connections. What has been your experience in this area?

5. Reflect on the companions' overall support in the area of spiritual reactions. Consider what was helpful and what was harmful about the type of support they provided. Reflecting on Job 42:7-9, what are your thoughts about how God perceived the companions' support in this area? What can Job's narrative teach us about being more supportive in the area of spiritual reactions?

6. Reflect on what role, if any, spiritual practises or traditions such as prayer, reading the Psalms or quoting Scripture played in the support the companions provided Job. Reflect on how these spiritual practises might or might not be helpful in providing comfort, especially when a sufferer is experiencing confused spiritual reactions.

7. Reflect on the degree to which the miserable comforters addressed or provided support for Job in the area of his physical reactions. Consider how their behavior likely impacted Job's recovery. What benefits might there be for the sufferer when someone makes consoling and empathetic responses to how they are doing physically?

8. Think about your own experiences with suffering. What types of grief responses did you experience and how did you or others respond to these reactions? Looking back, reflect on how these responses helped or hindered your grieving process.

Chapter Six
Consolation. Some Practical Responses

"As for you, you whitewash with lies; all of you are worthless physicians. If you would only keep silent, that would be your wisdom!" (13:4-5).

"I have heard many such things; miserable comforters are you all. Have windy words no limit? Or what provokes you that you keep on talking? I also could talk as you do if you were in my place; I could join words together against you, and shake my head at you. I could encourage you with my mouth, and the solace of my lips would assuage your pain" (16:2-5).

We have been exploring the importance of self-awareness and building a framework and context for understanding loss and grief. Although this is a critical foundation, becoming a consoling comforter is about more than just having self-awareness and head knowledge. It is about how we take that awareness and knowledge and put it into action. It is about how we embody that knowledge and exemplify empathy as we walk through our own grief and seek to comfort others.

The invitation to enter into adversity and to comfort a sufferer can be intimidating. There are many reasons we might feel uneasy or unnerved about entering into painful stories. Oftentimes, it is because we lack an understanding of loss and grief. Sometimes it may be because we are unsure about what we should say or do. We might lack confidence around the basic, practical skills of comforting. Or, because we are like the miserable companions and we prefer control and predictability and prosperity, suffering can be threatening to us.

The companions demonstrate how the human love of talking and trying to control the conversation and situation will often supersede the need to listen. Scripture repeatedly highlights the danger of us giving in to this temptation to speak more than we listen. Whenever someone dominates a discussion, refuses to listen, lectures, interrupts, is hasty with their words or is disrespectful, it destroys the safety of that conversation and wounds the other person and the relationship.

The companions exhibit how easy it is to give in to this temptation to speak, rather than to carefully, empathetically listen. Their need to argue their ideas and enforce their opinions overrode Job's need to be listened to. The urgency to hold onto their belief system shaped the conversation and turned them into miserable comforters.

This chapter examines some basic skills and practical acts of service. Ideally, the chapter will cultivate an awareness of some basic communication skills that help us to grow in our capacity to provide consoling comfort.

Before we start, it is important to clarify that it is *not* a comforter's responsibility to fix a sufferer's problems or manage their grief reactions. It is the sufferer's responsibility to work through their grief, and it is part of God's job description to help them. The comforter's role is to step into the spaces of suffering so that they can provide companionship and accountability, listen, offer compassion and encouragement. Ideally, consolation should open up the safe spaces for the sufferer to share and process their grief, clearing the way for God and the Holy Spirit to work.

In Job's narrative, it is obvious how the companions were more focused on sharing their thoughts than listening to what Job was trying to communicate. Their speeches were characterized by demeaning, dismissive, directive language. Their responses created such a hostile atmosphere, it denied Job a safe space to explore and process his grief. In Job's desperation to be heard, he pleaded with them to stop talking and just listen.

Speaker:	Comment:	Scripture Verse:
Job	"…all of you are worthless physicians. If only you would keep silent, that would be your wisdom! Hear now my reasoning, and listen to the pleading of my lips."	13:4-6
Job	"Let me have silence, and I will speak…"	13:13
Job	"Listen carefully to my words, and let my declaration be in your ears."	13:17
Job	"How long will you torment me, and break me in pieces with words?"	19:2
Job	"Listen carefully to my words, and let this be your consolation. Bear with me, and I will speak; then after I have spoken, mock on."	21:2-3

The Art of Active Listening.

The body of Job's narrative is focused on the conversations between Job and his companions. While one companion was speaking, the reader might assume that the others were listening. And perhaps they were listening to a degree, for they remained quiet.

However, when we study the content of the companions' speeches, it is evident that while the companions remained quiet while Job was speaking, they were not wholly listening to him. We can ascertain this from the content of their speeches. Their speeches were composed of their viewpoints and telling Job what to do and what to believe. They rarely acknowledged what Job was trying to communicate to them. This suggests that although the companions were hearing, they were so preoccupied with their own thoughts and purposes that they missed listening to what Job was trying to explain.

There is a very important distinction between hearing and listening. We can hear what someone is saying, or we can listen with intent and try to understand what they are trying to communicate. The *Spiritual Care Series* describes the difference between hearing and listening this way:

> "...hearing is the physical act of sound entering the ear and resonating on the eardrum," whereas "Listening is the assimilation of those physical sounds and their accompanying body language with one's own experience and integrating it into the present experience to give those sounds meaning and voice."[1]

It is so easy to be just like the miserable companions. Hearing someone talk, but not entirely listening to them. Remaining quiet, giving the appearance of listening, but our minds are adrift or elsewhere, distracted by something that is going on around us, thinking about how to resolve the issues or preparing our responses.

In contrast, active listening is a basic communication skill that helps us to *listen*, to understand and to hold onto what the speaker is saying. It lets the sufferer choose the topics, set the pace and the direction for the conversation. It helps us keep our focus on the sufferer. It is characterized by empathy, respect, and patience. And it affirms that we have been listening to what someone has been sharing.

While the comforter should participate in the conversation, it should not be through stating platitudes or clichés, or giving long-winded speeches that take over the conversation. Nor should it be to prove a point or to argue a theological stance. Rather, the ideal is concise, intentional responses that seek to clarify what we think the sufferer was trying to communicate or that encourages them to pursue their line of thought.

Active listening is an indispensable basic communication skill in the pursuit of providing consoling comfort because it validates what a sufferer is trying to communicate and helps them to sort through their whirling thoughts. Listening, and communicating that we are listening, affirms their personal worth and the value of their individual story.

Listening is a far more complex and demanding skill than most of us realize. While listening is most commonly described as being quiet and paying attention, there is actually much more to the art of listening. Listening takes discipline and concentrated effort. The listener has to prevent their thoughts from drifting. They have to conquer their desire to talk and interject. It is an art that is composed of skills, intentionality, empathy, and forbearance.

Even with all my counselling training and experience, it can still be hard for me to just listen. I can get so enthused about something that has been said that I leap in before the speaker is finished. I allow my excitement to override their right to speak and finish their thought. I also confess that I can be like the miserable comforters and try to convince someone of something, rather than sit with them in the spaces of their confusion or discomfort or hurt. This most often happens with people I love and deeply care about. People like my husband, children and daughters-in-law. When my heart gets tugged by something they are telling me, I immediately want to ease their heartache by fixing the problem. Too quickly, I try to rescue them from their pain and shift them to safety. It can be so hard on my momma's heart to see them hurting!

But the encouraging news is that these listening skills can be learned, and with practice, they can help us to become more attentive, engaged and empathetic. They also help us to become more observant about what the speaker is communicating through their non-verbal behavior.

Collins builds on this discussion when he describes active listening as being "more than giving passive or half-hearted attention to the words that come from another person. Effective listening is an active process. It involves:

o Being able to set aside your own conflicts, biases, and preoccupations so you can concentrate on what the other [sufferer] is communicating.

o Avoiding subtle verbal or non-verbal expressions of disapproval or judgement about what is being said, even when the content is offensive or shocking.

o Using both your eyes and your ears to detect messages that come from the tone of voice, pace of talking, ideas that are repeated, posture, gestures, facial expressions, and other clues apart from what the [sufferer] is saying.

o Hearing not only what the other person is saying, but noticing what gets left out.

o Noticing the sufferer's physical characteristics and general appearance, such as grooming and dress.

o Waiting patiently through periods of silence or tears as the [sufferer] summons enough courage to share something painful or pauses to collect his or her thoughts and regains composure.

o Looking at the [sufferer] as he or she speaks, but without either staring or letting our eyes wander around the room.

o Even though you may not condone his or her actions, values, or beliefs, you can always accept him or her. Sometimes, it can be helpful to imagine yourself in the [sufferer's] situation and attempt to see things from his or her point of view."[2]

And while it is not advisable for the comforter to share lengthy stories or engage in protracted explanations or teaching, there may be points where it is appropriate to share a personal anecdote to illustrate an idea. But these anecdotes must be timely and restricted to a few brief, relevant and purposeful statements.

The way a listener responds will influence the direction of the conversation. Even when their comments or observations are brief, what is said will highlight a certain idea, a feeling or theme which will prompt the speaker to explore them further. In this way, active listening can be very effective in drawing out the sufferer's unconscious or repressed thoughts and emotions or help them to pursue a line of thought, which might otherwise go unrecognized, unspoken, unexplored, and unresolved.

Job's narrative also teaches some realities about listening and talking. In all likelihood, we are like the companions, desiring to talk more than listen. We often seek to prove our point, wanting the sufferer to see things from our perspective. We are tempted to move them out of hurt places and into safe places far too quickly. We want to re-write their stories of loss with what we think are healthier perspectives, different interpretations, and happier endings. As a result, we can end up being just like the miserable companions and dominate the conversations, interrupting, criticizing, preaching or moralizing.

I am sure we can all admit that there are many times we have not been fully attentive when someone was talking to us. We can be miserable companions—people who speak more than listen. Discourage, more than encourage. But today, we can find a better way.

Non-Verbal Listening Responses

There are a few non-verbal listening responses that can help a comforter keep focused on the sufferer and let them know that they are indeed listening.

The comforter's physical posture is important. Turning one's body towards the sufferer, remaining still, and facing them with an open, relaxed posture communicates attentiveness and a willingness to listen.

Facial expressions and eye contact are other non-verbal ways that feelings and intentions are communicated. In his book, *The Art of Listening in a Healing Way*, James E. Miller writes that there is no part of the human body that is more expressive than our face and our eyes,

"...with its intricate weave of muscles, the human face can display more than 8,000 expressions, and it can do so in a fraction of a second...Almost faster, but not quite, for your eyes do catch these nuances and pass them on to be received as information for your brain...3

Based on our own experiences, we know the truth of Miller's assertion that we all communicate through our facial expressions. We just have to think about the teacher who raised their eyebrow at our answer, the parent who glared when we misbehaved or the friend whose face lit up in a smile when they spotted us. Not one of these people had to say a word, yet they conveyed a message that we received and understood.

Miller's observation about the expressiveness of our face and eyes is important with respect to providing comfort for three main reasons. First, when we face a sufferer, maintain eye contact and keep our facial expressions as relaxed and empathetic as possible, we communicate to them that we are listening and do care about what they are saying. This open posture will encourage the sufferer and allow them to keep sharing. Second, when a comforter becomes conscious of how much communication happens through our eyes, facial expressions, and other non-verbal behaviors such as the tone, volume and speed of their speech, and their "gestures and gait, [their] poses and postures," they can become more careful about these channels of communication.4 Finally, they can become more watchful of their own non-verbal behavior and start noticing the sufferer's facial and non-verbal expressions that leak what they are feeling.

Silence is another powerful non-verbal listening skill. Miller writes, "Silence is much more than a backdrop. It reaches toward the speaker and asks, 'Do you have more to say? Please go ahead.' A welcoming quietness issues an invitation: 'Do you wish to go deeper? I will go with you.' This easygoing stillness gives permission to the other person, 'You can say whatever you want and it will be accepted, just as you will be.'"5

Finally, the use of non-verbal gestures such as nodding, leaning in, and when appropriate, putting a hand on the shoulder or vocalizations such as, "mmm," "a-hum," "uh-huh," "a-ha," "I see," and "yes" are ways to communicate that we are listening and being attentive. Peel affirms that while these may seem like simple responses, they are powerful ways to encourage the sufferer to continue sharing.6

Empathy and Empathetic Responses

Another basic listening skill is the empathetic or reflective response. Even though it is referred to as a response, it is actually a listening skill because its intent is to affirm that the comforter has been attentive and wants to ensure that they have listened and heard correctly what the sufferer has been trying to communicate.

Empathetic responses are short, succinct phrases. They are used by the listener to restate or summarize what they think they have heard the speaker say. They can also be used to reflect back to the speaker what has been observed in their non-verbal behavior. Miller writes that these responses are "a paraphrase of what's been said, using your own wording, as a way of confirming the other's message" and encouraging them to continue sharing.7

These short reflective statements are always delivered in a gentle and tentative manner so that they come across as nurturing rather than definitive, critical or judgmental.

Some examples of basic empathetic responses include,

- "It seems like you are feeling _____ and _____ right now."

- "Since your loss, it sounds like it has been hard for you to _____."

- "I'm hearing that you're feeling _____ by all that has happened."

- "Losing _____ has contributed to your feeling _____."

- "You're feeling _____."

- "It sounds like you are feeling _____."

- "You're _____."

- "As I was listening to you, I sensed that you are feeling _____ about _____."

- "It seems that thinking about how your loss has _____, and these thoughts are making you feel _____."

- "As you were talking, I noticed that you were_____, and it made me think you are feeling_____."

- "I sense you have more to say about this..."

- "What might it mean that you feel so_____?"

- That must be hard.

From these examples, it is clear that the comforter tries not to add any of their own thoughts, feelings or perceptions to the response. Rather the responses are more like a mirror that reflects back to the sufferer what the comforter thinks they have seen and heard them say.

The beauty of these simple phrases is that they open up the receptive, safe spaces for the sufferer to share and explore their thoughts and feelings. When I was doing my first counselling practicum and used active listening for the first time with a client, I was shocked at how these simple responses open the door for the client to keep sharing. I remember when I used a simple reflective phrase in response to what had been shared, something along the lines of, "It sounds like you are feeling hurt," It was like the flood gates opened. Their words and emotions poured out. My simple show of empathy validated that I had listened, which then encouraged them to share in more expansive and profound ways.

I also remember another time where I made a reflective response to what I thought I heard a teenager telling me. I responded to him by saying, "You are very angry about what happened..." and he immediately replied, "No! I am not angry! I am pissed off!" As I had listened to him, I thought I'd picked up on how he had been impacted emotionally by the event. But when I reflected back to him what I thought I had heard him say, it turned out that I had not got it quite right. He was more deeply impacted than I had understood him to be. Nevertheless, my reflective comment gave him the opportunity to clarify how profoundly he had been impacted.

This is the beautiful thing about these simple reflective phrases. They help us to briefly summarize what we think we've heard. Sometimes we will get it right. Other times, we will be off the mark and miss what they are trying to tell us. But regardless, a reflective comment affirms that we have been listening and are trying to understand. They also open the spaces for the sufferer to be more specific, descriptive and open. In turn, this allows the comforter to get a better picture of what the sufferer is trying to express.

A timeless truth is the human tendency to talk and to be listened to, rather than to listen to someone else talk. This ends up meaning that few are willing and prepared to genuinely listen. I think this tendency has become even more pronounced in our current digital and social media culture, where there seems to be less real life connections than ever before. Today, the preferred mode of communication is through social media and emails. While these forms of communication may offer efficiency and quick solutions, they have largely replaced the meaningful, authentic and honest conversation that ensure people feel seen and heard. As a result, when someone needs to unburden themselves, they will likely find more miserable comforters then consoling comforters.

As I have worked with clients over the years, one of their most prevalent needs is to have someone to talk to and someone who will just listen to them. Clients regularly expressed their profound appreciation for having someone to talk to about anything, without fear of judgement, condemnation, dismissal or minimization. Being able to tell our stories and have someone listen is a transformative experience. As comforters, it is possible to do this for a sufferer. To be physically present. To listen. To use some basic communication skills that let the sufferer know that we see them, and we care deeply about what they are trying to communicate.

Appendix E offers two opportunities to practice making empathetic statements. It uses statements that Job made in his conversations with the companions. These activities can be done individually or as a group.

Open-ended Questions

In his speeches, God did not explicitly answer Job's questions, nor did he tell Job what to think. What he did do was use many rhetorical and open-ended questions. God's use of questions invited Job to think about what had been said and draw his own conclusions. His questions also stirred an emotional response within Job, which then motivated Job to engage with the questions. For it did not seem that God expected Job to immediately reply, because he asked them in quick succession and continued talking. But rather it seems that God intended his questions to help Job find greater clarity as he wrestled with finding answers to the questions he posed.

Tremper Longman, in his commentary *Job*, writes that it is "through God's constant questioning, Job came to realize the limits of his wisdom and knowledge. He tried to claim knowledge of the working of the universe that was vastly beyond him…God did not strictly operate the way Job thought. But now he has had a personal encounter with God, and his understanding is vastly expanded."[8]

Speaker:	Comment:	Scripture Verse:
God	"Where were you when I laid the foundation of the earth?"	38:4
God	"Have you entered into the springs of the sea, or walked in the recesses of the deep?"	38:16
God	"What is the way to the place where the light is distributed, or where the	38:24

	east wind is scattered upon the earth?"	
God	"Who has put wisdom in the inward parts, or given understanding to the mind?"	38:36
God	"Is it by your wisdom that the hawk soars, and spreads its wings towards the south?"	39:26
God	"Shall a faultfinder contend with the Almighty?"	40:2
God	"Have you an arm like God, and can you thunder with a voice like his?"	40:9

God's consummate use of questions illuminates the efficacy of asking well-phrased questions. They accomplished at least three outcomes. First, because God's questions related to what Job and his companions had been discussing, they confirmed that he had been listening to their conversations. Second, God used his questions to enter into the conversations and invite them to consider his points. Third, his questions were effective in energizing Job, his companions and the reader to think more deeply about all that had been raised.

When Job finally answers God, it is clear that he has reflected on all God's questions and observations. Through his contemplation, he has arrived at a new understanding of God and God's role in human suffering. Job's suffering had become a transformative experience and through it his theology had been refined. Job confesses to God that,

> "I know that you can do all things, and that no purpose of
> yours can be thwarted...Therefore I have uttered what I

did not understand, things too wonderful for me, which I did not know. I had heard of you by the hearing of the ear, but now my eye sees you..." (42:2-5).

Throughout the conversations, we can see that the companions also asked many questions.

Speaker:	Question:	Scripture Verse:
Eliphaz	"If one ventures a word with you, will you be offended?"	4:2
Bildad	"Does God pervert justice?"	8:3
Eliphaz	"Is not your wickedness great?"	22:5
Bildad	"How then can a mortal be righteous before God?"	25:4
Elihu	"If you are righteous, what do you give to him; or what does he receive from your hand?"	35:7
Elihu	"Do you know how God lays his command upon them, and causes the lightning of his cloud to shine?"	37:15

Questions can be described or classified as rhetorical, closed-ended or open-ended questions. The differences between these types of questions are significant.

Rhetorical questions are not asked in order to get an answer, but rather, they are intended to make a point, to trigger some thought or feeling about what has been said, and to persuade the listener to consider another way of looking at things.

Closed-ended questions are phrased in such a way that a sufferer can respond with one-word answers such as "yes," "no," "maybe" or "don't know." As a result, these questions can discourage further discussion. These questions are easy to identify because they usually start with words like "are," "do," "can," "will" or "did".

In contrast, open-ended questions are phrased in such a way that they compel a sufferer to provide more detailed responses and open up their communication. These questions tend to start with "who," "what," "where," "when," "why," or "how."

Questions that begin with "how" will encourage the sufferer to consider and talk about in what manner things have unfolded since the loss or how they are reacting in their grief.

Questions starting with "what" will prompt the sufferer to center on more factual things such as the details about what happened, things they want done regarding the funeral or specifics about what has been the most challenging tasks they have had to do as a result of their loss.

Questions that start with "when" or "where" will nudge the sufferer to consider things such as the timing, location or the sequence of events.

Questions beginning with "who" will invite the sufferer to reflect on aspects of their experience that relate to their social connections and social reactions.

Questions that begin with "why" will stir contemplation about possible reasons or explanations for something that happened. However, questions which begin with "why" must be used with caution because they can often come across as accusatory or condemning. They may make the sufferer feel like they have to explain, defend or justify their choices or grief reactions. Also, as we witnessed in Job's narrative, sometimes, it is impossible to get answers about why we have to face adversity. Some things just remain a mystery.

The goal of using questions when comforting someone is to encourage them to ponder a point or expand on something that they have shared. The key to asking effective questions is to ensure that they are used sparingly, in a non-judgemental, gentle manner so that they encourage the sufferer to keep sharing and to help them pursue a line of thought or a feeling.

Some examples of open-ended questions are:

- o "How did you respond to that?"
- o "What has this been like for you?"
- o "What can you remember about what happened?"
- o "Are there any Scripture verses that are sustaining you or giving you comfort?"
- o "Have you been experiencing God in any way throughout this challenging time?"
- o "In the middle of this, how can I or others best support you spiritually? Physically? Emotionally?"
- o "What thoughts and feelings have you been having around your spirituality or your faith?"
- o "Who do you find most comforting right now?"
- o "What were you thinking/feeling when _____?"

- o "What are some ways that you have been feeling depleted or energized?"

- o "Where are you able to see glimmers of hope?"

- o "It seems you are feeling confined to your home. Where are some places we could go to give you a break and a change of scenery?"

- o "I sense you are feeling helpless and hopeless right now. What can I do to help you? What have you already tried?"

- o "Have you ever had thoughts of hurting yourself as a way to escape the pain and grief?"

- o What are some ways that I can help you?

- o What do you need right now?

The intentional use of questions is an effective communication skill in suffering experiences. Questions help the comforter to stay focused on listening to what the sufferer is thinking, feeling and experiencing. Well-timed and well-phrased questions also invite the sufferer to reflect on a new line of thinking, highlight a concern or issue, expound further on some comment, adopt new insights, and help them to unknot their muddled thinking. Finally, as we observed in God's speeches, questions also affirm to the sufferer that we have been present and listening.

Appendix F offers three opportunities to practice creating and using open-ended questions in response to things that Job shared with the companions.

Less is More: Making Concise Observations

While Job's companions did make observations about Job's adversity, they tended to be long-winded, opinionated, argumentative, and confrontational observations. Their statements were intended to convince Job to maintain their theological viewpoints or to comply with their advice. When the companions became more insistent, Job became more resistant. When he refused to entertain their comments, their tempers flared, the conflict escalated, and a power struggle ensued. In the end, Job felt misunderstood and unsupported.

A more helpful communication skill or strategy would have been for the companions to use concise or succinct observations that kept the focus on Job and his grief experience. Hulme suggests that the use of concise observations would have been more likely to facilitate Job considering their perspective or acquiring an insight.9

A concise observation is a straightforward, succinct statement, offered in a tentative manner. It invites the sufferer to consider something that the comforter has noticed or discerned.

Prior to making an observation, the comforter must take the time to listen, observe, and study the situation. Collecting information ensures that there are sufficient grounds for the comment to be made. Observations are always best when they are made in gentle, respectful ways.

Perhaps one of the best ways of thinking about this skill is that it is like sowing a seed.10 The comforter's goal in making an observation is to plant a thought or perception regarding something they have noted. It then becomes the sufferer's responsibility to consider that piece of information and decide how they will respond and whether or not they will accept it. It is important to mention that while the sufferer may initially reject the observation, it is not uncommon for them to accept the idea later when they have had time to ponder it.

Some examples of how to phrase a concise observation are,

- o "Here is something I have noticed..." "Here is how I see it..." Or, "Here is another way you might look at it..."11

- o "Something I noticed as you have been talking is that _____."

- o "It seems you have concluded _____, but I wonder if you might consider seeing it from this angle_____?"

- o "Over the last few times we have visited, I have observed that _____."

- o "Another perspective might be _____."

- o "Perhaps it is possible to see it this way, _____."

- o "I invite you to think about it this way_____."

- o "Have you considered _____?"

Oftentimes comforters will feel the urge to make an observation that includes their sharing a similar experience that they or someone else has had. This leads to the comforter interjecting their story into the conversation. This is usually an easy thing to spot because it starts with something like, "I know what you are going through. The same thing happened to me...." or "The exact same thing happened to a friend of mine....," and then it moves into a lengthy description of the experience. There are a number of problems with this type of observation. It assumes that the comforter and the sufferer have experienced the same loss, in the same way. This is presumptuous because every loss has its own unique, nuanced grief reactions. No two suffering experiences are exactly alike. The distinctive nature of grief precludes anyone from presuming they know exactly what another person is experiencing.

Yet, there can be great value in a comforter sharing a part or a brief summary of their story. It can help the sufferer learn from another's experience and know that they are not alone in their suffering. However, the comforter must be very thoughtful about how and when to share a bit of their story. The observation must be relevant. It must be brief and purposeful. It should help the comforter communicate that they have a sense of what the sufferer is experiencing and that they have suffered in similar ways. Finally, an observation is best when it provides an insight that might be helpful to the sufferer.

A key to sharing a part of our story as a way to make an observation is that it must be concise, preferably only 4-5 statements maximum. It does not reflect the comforter's whole suffering story, but it is a few statements that share a theme or some of the main elements of their experience.

Also, as Paul Tripp recommends, rather than sharing an observation that centers solely on oneself, it is ideal when it highlights how God was the "key actor in the drama," drawing attention to how "our stories belong to him and point to him."[12] Keeping the focus on God's role in the story helps to illuminate how he has worked within our experiences. Tripp goes on to suggest that we should "tell the story with humility, admitting [our] continuing need for grace" and the resources that can only Christ can provide.[13] Our stories are best told in ways that highlight how "life is not defined by our pain but by our union with Christ."[14]

A simple frame for making an observation that includes part of one's narrative could be something along these lines:

- o Start with one introductory statement which clarifies that while it is impossible to know exactly what they are going through because everyone's narrative is unique, we have also walked through loss and grief.

- o A second statement that briefly mentions the type of loss(es).

- o A third statement mentions that we too struggled to find our way through the grief and,

- o A final statement or two which summarizes how God comforted us, met us in our suffering, worked within that loss and helped to sustain us.[15]

Appendix G offers a simple application exercise that can help with writing a short observation about a loss experience. It may be helpful for a comforter to compose a simple summary of a couple of aspects of your story using the prompts so that you will be ready to share them in a concise, appropriate, timely and encouraging way.

Showing Up. Acts of Service.

When someone is suffering, people typically want to reach out and do something to help. Oftentimes they think they have to help in some major way. Yet, as Fr. Joseph Tham writes in his article, "Communicating with Sufferers: Lessons from the Book of Job," the research has consistently shown that even very "small acts of service can make a huge difference."[16]

We observe these small, but powerful acts of service in Job's narrative when his companions initially showed up and entered into his grief. The gifts of their physical presence, companionship and sitting with him in silence were very comforting and affirming for Job. Their open expressions of grief also communicated their empathy and solidarity with Job's grief.

The companions' behaviour helps emphasize how simple acts of service and connection can help alleviate suffering. Tham affirms that, "This alone may often be what the afflicted need."[17]

Paul Tripp builds on this idea when he writes, "We offer people a living, loving presence that puts real flesh and blood on the presence of the Lord."[18] Donald Peel echoes this idea when he contends that a comforter should "… go with no other motive than to show that in Christ's love, you care enough to call on them. No ulterior motive. No hidden agenda. No other goal."[19]

Peel continues, "When a Christian visits [a sufferer], there is a real sense in which Christ himself has visited that person. When you walk into the sickroom, Christ walks in. There is no presumption in such a statement. Christ is there in the person of yourself, for you are a member of him, an extension of his Person."[20]

Showing up and being present are profound acts of service that reflect and embody Christ's love. Engaging in practical acts of service are other ways that a comforter can exemplify how Christ and his disciples served others, especially in their adversity.

Some examples of practical acts of service that comforters can provide:

- o Buy them a journal to write down their thoughts, emotions, struggles.
- o Help them make a memory book with photos and other elements so they tell a story of the deceased's life.

o Make a collage with cut-outs from magazines to represent the loved one's life, the griever's life or the relationship between the griever and the lost loved one.

o Help with self-care, such as encouraging them to take naps, shower, exercise/walk or have something to eat.

o Allow them to talk and tell their stories.

o Putting on some music can be healing and relaxing.

o Help them plan ahead for special days or holidays that might be difficult.

o Include them in activities and have them over for a meal or coffee.

o Help organize visits with others to ensure the sufferer has regular visits and companionship.

o Organize people/companions to write encouraging messages in cards that can be collected and then opened at times when the sufferer may feel particularly discouraged or alone.

o Taking them for walks in nature can be healing.

o Offer to help create some rituals that might honor the deceased.

o Hugs—but only after asking for permission. Asking permission first allows the sufferer to exercise control over their circumstances and bodies during a time when they have been unable to control what has happened. Asking permits them to decide if physical contact will comfort them or if it will disarm them and cause them to feel greater vulnerability.

o Share some memories and ask them to share some memories.

o Books on loss and grief might be offered when the timing seems appropriate.

o Offer to care for children or pets.

o Doing practical chores like the laundry, cutting the grass, watering the lawn, cleaning the house, running errands, buying groceries, or providing meals or making them coffee or tea.

o Offer to drive them to appointments.

o Offer to read Scripture for them and with them.

o Offer to pray with them and for them.

o Offer to write out some Scripture passages for them so that when they are particularly down or discouraged, they can quickly refer to them.

o Bring a plant or flowers. Or perhaps bring a shrub that can be planted in memorial.

o Offer to make phone calls or send messages to tell people and keep them informed.

o Offer to help prioritize tasks and decisions that have to be made and decide who might be able to assist with each task.

o When they are ready, and the timing is right, offer to help create an inventory of the ways God has been working in their life and what blessings they have experienced during this season of loss and grief.

The narrator does not mention whether Job's community, companions or wife engaged in any of these acts of service.

However, the reality is that practical acts of service do provide great comfort to a sufferer. When we show up and offer to help in concrete ways, we are consoling comforters.

When Another is Needed: Referrals

Collins aptly points out that "referrals are an acknowledgement that no one person has the time, stamina, emotional stability, knowledge, skill, or experience to help everyone."21

As a comforter walks alongside a sufferer, there may be a point where they sense that the sufferer's grief has become too prolonged, complicated or deep. These are occasions when it seems that the sufferer's grief has moved into depression or complex trauma. Or it seems they have become stuck or they are or thinking about engaging in some type of self-harming behavior. As we observe in Job's narrative, there are times where his extreme adversity and prolonged suffering created such despair that he loathed his life and hints or states his desire to die (3:11; 7:16; 9:21; 10:1, 21-22; 6:8-9). When a sufferer becomes so overwhelmed, exhausted or overextended emotionally, they may lack the insight, capacity or energy to pursue possible medical, counselling or professional support. All of these situations indicate that another may be needed, and it is time to suggest a referral(s).

As a result, the comforter may play a major role in discerning when another is needed, and a referral is necessary. When it appears that a referral might be warranted, the comforter can begin by making a concise observational statement and asking a few questions about what they have noticed. Then they can explain why they believe things have become worrisome. This can be followed up by simply stating that it would be wise to seek support from another who is more qualified, who has greater expertise and experience in this area. The comforter could then offer to help the sufferer by researching some possibilities or even help to make initial contact.

The comforter could also offer to assist the sufferer by driving and accompanying them into the appointment if necessary.

However, it is important to make two further points. First, prior to doing research or making a connection with another, it is respectful and empowering when the comforter first discusses it with the sufferer. Consultation allows the sufferer a measure of control in a situation where it may feel like they have lost control. It also allows a sufferer the opportunity to guide the process by weighing in on things like timing and choosing the person or the setting they prefer. In order to maintain confidentiality and trust, it is very important for the comforter to ask permission before sharing information or proceeding. If a sufferer's personal information is shared without their knowledge, they may feel betrayed, exposed, and trust could be broken. H. Norman Wright affirms the importance of maintaining confidentiality in his book, *Helping Those Who Hurt: Reaching Out to Your Friends in Need,* when he writes that "keeping confidences is foundational" in maintaining the sufferer's trust.22

When to Refer:

o When the sufferer seems stuck in the grief process for a prolonged period of time, and they have not returned to at least some of their regular activities, it is prudent that they see their family physician or a health care professional. Their doctor can provide a medical evaluation to determine if there is any underlying health issue(s) and, if necessary, offer medication or treatment. If warranted, the doctor could also make a further referral to a medical specialist, a registered clinical counsellor, or a psychologist who is specialized in loss and grief and trauma work.

o If the sufferer is a student, it is advisable to notify the school or university counsellor about what has been observed and the concerns. This ensures that they can provide additional support and comfort and keep a watchful eye out for the sufferer's well-being.

o Whenever a comforter notices that there are any concerns around a legal issue, the sufferer should be encouraged to consult a lawyer for legal advice.

o Whenever a comforter notices there might be financial issues, it is important to encourage them to seek financial advice from someone at their bank or a financial planner who can provide them expert financial advice.

o Whenever a sufferer has unresolved questions around their faith, theology, and God's role in their suffering, a referral to their pastor/ minister/ priest and to a spiritual advisor would be highly recommended.

o If there are possible signs of addiction with alcohol, drugs or gambling, referrals could include seeking medical help, accessing self-help groups such as Alcoholics or Narcotics or Gambling Anonymous, seeing a registered clinical counsellor or joining a community support group that specializes in these areas.

o When the sufferer expresses feeling all alone in their suffering, a referral to a community, or a church bereavement support group might be suggested.

o It is an urgent concern whenever a sufferer hints or speaks about self-harming or hurting another person. Asking simple, open-ended and closed questions can help to clarify exactly what they are thinking or intending and can help to determine the degree or level of risk. It is imperative to make an immediate response to any such worrisome comments or hints because it may indicate the sufferer's or another person's safety or life may be at risk.

o This latter situation warrants an immediate contact to be made with a medical professional, a hospital emergency room, calling an ambulance or the local police depending on the nature, degree and immediacy of the risk and danger.

However, if the threat to self or others is imminent, then the sufferer must get to the nearest hospital emergency room and the police need to be involved immediately.

Contacting the non-emergency RCMP line, the non-emergency ambulance line, or the 24-Hour Crisis Line can be very helpful in these circumstances. All of these services have trained personnel to help the comforter determine the level of risk and offer suggestions about the best way to handle the situation.

It is important to mention that in crisis situations, it is permissible to break confidentiality, if necessary. The sufferer's and others' safety and wellbeing are a priority in these situations, and efforts must be made to prevent anyone's safety, health, or life being put at risk.

A List of Possible Non-Emergency Referrals and **Possible Emergency Referrals** have been provided in Appendix H.

Reflections and Applications

1. While active listening sounds easy, it is actually quite hard. Oftentimes, we want to speak more than we want to listen to someone else.

Reflect on your experiences with listening and consider if you have had any experiences with someone who truly listened to you. Reflect on what it was like to be heard.

Reflect on how well you actively listen and specific ways you might improve in this area.

Reflect on Job's companions and consider how well they actively listened to Job and how they may have responded differently.

2. Complete the activity in Appendix I that focuses on engaging in acts of service. Use the exercise and the list of possible activities to consider whether Job's companions provided consolation in this area. Reflect on how each act might have helped to alleviate Job's suffering.

Reflect on how physical acts of service have played out in your life. Have you ever been a recipient of such service? If so, what was it like to experience such gifts of service?

Alternatively, have you ever engaged in such acts of service, and if so, what was your sense about how others received them?

3. Reflect on what you have learned about active listening, open-ended questions, and making observations and consider whether the miserable comforters used any of these simple communication strategies in their conversations with Job.

Review Collins' description of active listening and the list of things it involves. As you review the list, consider which of them comes naturally to you and which ones you could improve on.

4. Reflect on the difference between closed and open-ended questions. Consider how you might use them in conversation and how they might aid in listening and providing comfort.

5. Reflect on what concerns or hesitations you may have about suggesting a referral or that may even prevent you from pursuing a referral for someone. Reflect on ways you might overcome any concerns about making a referral to another.

6. How might a comforter engage in self-care when they are supporting a sufferer?

How might they care for themselves when they are asked to hold someone's story confidential?

What are some ways we could communicate to a sufferer that while they still care for them, we are currently not in a place to provide support?

Chapter Seven
Consolation. Some Theological Responses

"Why did I not die at birth, come forth from the womb and expire? Why were there knees to receive me, or breasts for me to suck? Now I would be lying down and quiet; I would be asleep; then I would be at rest..." (3:11-13).

"...and the Lord accepted Job's prayer. And the Lord restored the fortunes of Job when he had prayed for his friends..." (42:9-10).

Use of Scripture and Theology

Job inquires, "But where shall wisdom be found? And where is the place of understanding?" (28:12). He later answers his own question by stating, "God understands the way to it, and he knows its place" and "...'Truly, the fear of the Lord, that is wisdom..." (28:23, 28). By the epilogue, Job had discerned that wisdom was to be found in God and his word.

The prophet Isaiah echoed Job's view when he described God's word as being like rain that soaks the parched land (Isa 55:1-13). His beautiful imagery conveys how God's word can be like giving water to the thirsty, providing wisdom for the human mind.

John Patton, in his book, Pastoral Care, An Essential Guide, considers God's word specifically in relationship to suffering and consolation, when he writes, "the books of the Bible known as the Wisdom literature—Job, Proverbs, and Ecclesiastes—can be a resource for developing both personal and pastoral wisdom."1 Patton continues this train of thought when he asserts how it "is the very human quality of these books that can offer important guidance for the ministry of pastoral care."2

However, whenever God's word is used carelessly, superficially, or incorrectly, it can end up being hurtful rather than restorative. This occurred in Job's narrative when the companions used God's word and their theology to prove their points and reprimand Job. Derek Kidner contends in his book, The Wisdom of Proverbs, Job & Ecclesiastes, that the "basic error of Job's friends is that they overestimate their grasp of truth, misapply the truth they know, and closed their minds to any facts that contradict what they assume."3

Because the companions rigidly applied their theology, they ended up misrepresenting God, misjudging Job, and wounding rather than consoling him. Their words were so excruciating that Job rebuked them and pleaded with them to stop, "How long will you torment me, and break me into piece with words?" (19:2) In the epilogue, God also rebukes the companions for not having spoken of him rightly, as his servant Job had (42:7).

It is a timeless and cross-cultural truth that the way God's word is used in suffering and consolation, it can be either soothing and enriching or vexing and injurious.

In his book, *How Do I Help a Hurting Friend?*, Rod J. K. Wilson offers guidance around the use of Scripture when he writes, "When people are in the midst of grief, particularly the early stages, they do not need biblical exegesis or systematic theology. What they need instead is the presence of Christ, and the work of the Holy Spirit demonstrated through our presence."4

Timothy Keller expands Wilson's point when he contends that,

"There is a way of using theology and theological arguments that wounds rather than heals. This is not the fault of theology and theological arguments; it is the fault of the "miserable comforter" who fastens on an inappropriate fragment of truth, or whose timing is off, or whose attitude is condescending, or whose application is insensitive, or whose true theology is couched in such culture-laden clichés that they grate rather than comfort."[5]

Drawing upon these insights, it is clear that when a comforter is thinking about quoting a verse or discussing Scripture as a way to provide comfort, they must be discerning about what, when, and how to share. John Patton offers sage advice when he suggests that the comforter must first "listen in order to be present and to understand the situation of the person cared for so that what is offered as guidance will be specific to that person, not something that might be said or suggested to anyone."[6] Patton's suggestion is a notable reminder that the comforter's first task is to listen to understand so that they can then discern a relevant verse and determine whether there is an opportune time to share it.

Discernment about what might be relevant and consoling requires that the comforter begins with patience and attentive listening. Then the comforter ought to consider the question, "What verse might best apply to the sufferer's situation?"

The comforter should always ask permission before referencing Scripture or introducing a theological concept. Checking first will help to determine the sufferer's faith tradition and spirituality or whether they are even in a place to hear God's Word. Whenever a sufferer feels distant from God or is confused about their faith, they may resent or resist having his word inserted into their suffering.

The comforter can also gently probe whether the sufferer has been turning to Scripture, and if so, what verses they have found to be comforting. Not only will this help the comforter to gauge the sufferer's readiness to engage with Scripture, but it will reveal the passages and themes that have been resonating with the sufferer.

The Psalms can be particularly helpful in providing comfort during times of sorrow because they deal with every human emotion and experience. The Book of Job and Lamentations are also excellent extended treatises that offer ancient wisdom about God and human suffering and lament.

The Gift of Restorative Grace

The companions became miserable comforters when they kept referencing their reward and retribution theology as a way to explain Job's adversity. They were stuck on the idea that Job was being punished because he had sinned, and he could regain his prosperity by repenting. Their responses reflected the concept of retribution, where poor choices lead to consequences and punishment. In his book entitled *Rebuilding Your Broken World*, Gordon MacDonald describes this concept of retribution as "repayment in kind or punishment or the demand for reparations."[7] Chandra Gunawan in her article, "Retribution in the Wisdom Literature and Tradition," adds to this discussion when she describes how the theme of retribution in the Old Testament was as understood as the wicked suffering in proportion to their wickedness.[8]

Speaker:	Comment:	Scripture Verse:
Eliphaz	"Think now, who that was innocent ever perished? Or where were the upright cut off?"	4:7
Bildad	"Does God pervert justice? Or does the Almighty pervert the right?"	8:3
Zophar	"For he knows those who are worthless; when he sees iniquity, will he not consider it?"	11:11
Zophar	"Do you not know this from of old, ever since mortals were placed on earth, that the exulting of the wicked is short, and the joy of the godless is but for a moment? This is the portion of the wicked from God, the heritage decreed for them by God."	20:4, 29
Zophar	"If you direct your heart rightly, you will stretch out your hands towards him. If iniquity is in your hand, put it far away, and do not let wickedness reside in your tents."	11:13-14
Eliphaz	"If you return to the Almighty, you will be restored, if you remove unrighteousness from your tents…then you will delight yourself in the Almighty, and lift up your face to God."	22:23, 26

Yet, in the epilogue, we observe a different type of concept in play—the concept of restorative grace. We first notice it when God commands the companions to go to his servant Job and make sacrifices, as an act of contrition, and Job would pray for them, despite the fact they had contributed to Job's pain and had done little to deserve his prayers or forgiveness. When Job obeyed and prayed on behalf of his companions, God accepted his prayers and did not deal with the companions according to their folly. The concept of restorative grace appears once again when Job forgave his community and welcomed them into his home. The narrator describes this restorative action when he writes, "Then there came to him all his brothers and sisters and all who had known him before, and they ate bread with him in his house…" (42:11).

Job's willingness to forgive both his companions and community was driven by the concept of restorative grace, which Gordon MacDonald describes as an "…action to forgive the misbehavior and draw the broken-world person back toward wholeness and usefulness again."9 Restorative grace cannot be earned or purchased, but only freely given and freely accepted.

MacDonald writes, "in its primary sense, grace (literally meaning 'gift') is the power of God in the form of forgiving and healing love; it comes to men and women despite the fact that they have done nothing to deserve it."10 So, from a Christian perspective, grace begins with the free gift of forgiveness and restoration offered through Jesus's sacrifice on the Cross. When we accept Jesus's invitation to follow him and accept his gift of forgiveness and grace, we are then invited to extend the same forgiveness and grace to others, including the sinner, the outcast, the betrayer, the unfortunate. People who are broken and suffering. Just like us.

Tremper Longman contends that God restored Job's prosperity *after* Job prayed for his companions and when "he works for the restoration of the people who had been so hard on him. The restoration begins with his family and friends, all of whom had distanced themselves from him when he was in distress (6:14-23; 19:13-22). But now they are reconciled with him, even before God restores his material prosperity."11

Yet, it remains true that most of us can find it difficult to offer grace, forgiveness and comfort to someone who has caused their own suffering. Whenever we fixate on their poor choice(s) their suffering will be perceived as being merited and justified and deserved. This can cause us to feel irritated, impatient, frustrated or angry with them for what they have done or not done. We can become like the miserable comforters and find ourselves being pulled into the trap of retribution thinking (they must be guilty and deserve the consequences), drifting into criticism and lacking compassion for their plight.

Another enduring truth is that whenever we make a judgement about someone's story of suffering, it reveals that we think we are on a higher moral ground, and somehow are more righteous, more moral, or more ethical than they are. The underlying implication is that we have not and would not ever make such poor choices. That their poor choices are worse than the poor choices that we have made and the poor choices we will continue to make. We see these assumptions play out when companions acted out of a sense of their own morality, self-righteousness, and unfairly and unjustly judged Job for his presumed sins.

Yet, if we are willing to cast our eyes inward rather than outward, becoming self-referenced rather than other-referenced in terms of sin and poor choices, we will come to the realization that we are in no place to judge or criticize others. Evaluating our own behavior breaks down the illusion that we are *always* ethical, moral, honorable. For honest self-assessment will uncover the multiple times where we also made poor decisions that contributed to merited suffering in our own lives. We come face to face with how we have fallen short of God's best for us. Our blinders are removed. Pride and presumptions are stripped away. And it is here that we meet God and receive the gifts of his abundant mercy and grace.

Genuine introspection is a humbling process. But once we are able to face our own sin, we become less prone to judge others. And it is from this place that we become capable of offering restorative grace to others and to ourselves.

A few years ago, my husband and I began to include confessional prayers in our morning devotional and prayer time. Initially, we were quite confident that we would only have a few things to confess each morning. We were equally sure that over time our lists would grow shorter as we became more aware of the places we were falling short. But what we soon discovered was that our lists did not grow shorter. They actually grew longer! As we started to pay attention, we began catching just how often we were falling into temptation, making poor choices, disobeying God's call and expectations for our lives. I have found confession and repentance to be a very humbling practice. But we have also experienced some beautiful things as a result of doing this practice. Every day we experienced God's amazing forgiveness and grace. Every day we were able to offer grace and compassion to one another. We have started to see ourselves in a more authentic, honest, compassionate way. As we removed our masks of perfection and pride and stopped pretending we had everything all figured out, we have found greater freedom and joy. And in the end, we are growing in our ability to offer restorative grace and forgiveness towards all others.

At the end of Job's narrative, we witness Job coming to this place of humility. Derek Kidner describes it as, "Job has no such pretensions any longer. Seeing God with newly opened eyes, he has no questions, only a confession and a self-abasement that is as deep as his indignation had been high."12 We see this transformation in Job's confession, "...Therefore I have uttered what I did not understand, things too wonderful for me, which I did not know... I had heard of you by the hearing of the ear, but now my eye sees you; therefore I despise myself, and repent in dust and ashes" (42:3, 5).

Job's narrative invites us to live out of restorative grace. We saw how this worked in Job's narrative. After Job experienced God's benevolence, he became capable of showing forgiveness and grace towards his companions and the community that had mocked, demeaned and abandoned him. Restorative grace healed his relationships and restored his community.

God's restorative grace continues to have the mighty power to heal. To forgive. To show mercy. To mend our brokenness. To transform us. To repair our relationships. So that we can live out of that restorative grace and offer it to others.

Prayer: In God's Presence.

Prayer is deliberate, honest communication with God. It is about both listening to God and talking to God.

In *Christian Discourses*, Søren Kierkegaard contended that listening is a critical component of prayer when he wrote, "A man prayed, and at first he thought that prayer was talking. But he became more and more quiet until in the end he realized that prayer is listening."13

I thought Kierkegaard's observation was interesting, specifically in relationship to our discussion. We have talked about how Job pleaded with his companions to stop talking and just listen to him. We also have discussed how being present and just listening to a sufferer creates the sacred spaces where they can feel valued and listened to. Kierkegaard's comment is a great reminder that not only is listening important in terms of our horizontal relations and providing comfort to others, but it is also important in terms of our prayer and our vertical relationship with God. Remaining silent in prayer creates the spaces for God to speak and for us to listen. I imagine there are just as many times God yearns for us to be quiet, just as Job implored the miserable comforters to stop talking, and listen and to him.

Because prayer is an avenue for us to both hear from God and to with communicate with God, it can have a compelling role to play in suffering and in providing consolation. The Book of Job illuminates several ways we can try to communicate with God in our suffering.

Tham points out that Job and Elihu spoke directly to God as they prayed, as they searched for him, challenged and questioned him, and sought to understand his role in Job's adversity.14 In contrast, Eliphaz, Zophar and Bildad remain focused on talking about God and their theology but never actually turned to prayer.15 And as God points out in the epilogue, Job had spoken accurately about God and to God, even in his lament.

A comforter can also use prayer to prepare their thoughts and heart prior to providing consolation. However, before a comforter actually prays for or with the sufferer, it is always wise to first ask the sufferer whether they would like prayer and, if so, what they might like to have included. Letting the sufferer make decisions about prayer communicates sensitivity to where they are in regard to their faith, spirituality and suffering journey.

Scripture is saturated with the encouragement to pray unceasingly, in all circumstances:

- o "Pray in the Spirit at all times in every prayer and supplication" (Eph 6:18).

- o "...pray without ceasing..." (1 Thess 5: 17).

- o "Devote yourself to prayer..." (Col 4:2).

- o "...persevere in prayer." (Rom 12:12),

- o "... pray always..." (Lk 18:1).

- o "Are any among you suffering? They should pray. Are any cheerful? They should sing songs of praise. Are any among you sick? They should call for the elders of the church and have them pray over them, anointing them with oil in the name of the Lord. The prayer of faith will save the sick, and the Lord will raise them up; and anyone who has committed sins will be forgiven. Therefore confess your sins to one another, and pray for one another, so that you may be healed. The prayer of the righteous is powerful and effective" (Jas 5:13-18).

Hulme concurs that even in the darkest situations and adversity, prayers have the power to foster hope, faith and peace.[16] April Yamasaki, in her book, *Four Gifts: Seeking Self-Care for Heart, Soul, Mind and Strength* expands upon this observation when she shares that "research today indicates that prayer can also play a significant role in maintaining our mental, emotional, physical, and spiritual health."[17]

H. Norman Wright contends that "praying accomplishes several things. It releases [the sufferer] to God, and it reminds us that we are not the ones who are the final resource in this life," it helps people become more conscious of God's presence, it is a way to ask for God for guidance and insight, and it affirms that the comforter has been attentive to the sufferer's concerns and issues.18

Job turned to prayer and to God in his suffering season. When Job was informed of his traumatic losses, he "arose, tore his robe, shaved his head, and fell on the ground and worshipped (1:20). As he worked through his grief, he continued to turn to God in prayer and lament. And in the epilogue, Job prayerfully interceded for his companions.

Timothy Keller writes,

> "Through it all, Job never stopped praying. Yes, he complained, but he complained to *God*. He doubted, but he doubted to *God*. He screamed and yelled, but he did it in God's presence. No matter how much agony he was in, he continued to address God. Hekept seeking him. And in the end, God said Job triumphed. How wonderful that our God sees the grief and anger and questioning and is still willing to say 'you triumphed'—not because it was all fine, not because Job's heart and motives were always right,but because Job's doggedness in seeking the face and presence of God meant that the *suffering did not drive him away from God but toward him.* And that made all the difference."19

One of the key points in Keller's passage is that while Job prayed and lamented, screamed and yelled, "he did it in God's presence." This reminds us that whatever we think, say and do, and whenever we pray, it is always in the presence of God.

Yet, we notice in Job's narrative that while God is omniscient, always present, he sometimes chooses to remain silent. And he sometimes refuses to answer our prayers or questions. So, there are times when it may seem to a sufferer that God has abandoned them, is not listening or willing to answer their prayers. We observe this happen in Job's narrative when God was silent through the conversations, and Job wondered where he was. And then when God did speak, he never specifically answered Job's questions or addressed Job's prayers. Keller continues, God "withhold[s] the full story from Job, even after the test was over, keeps him walking by faith, not by sight. He does not say in the end, 'Now I see it all.' He never sees it all. He sees God" (42:5).**20**

Even though God never answered Job's specific questions about why he was suffering, Job eventually found reassurance in knowing that God is sovereign and good and just. Job witnessed God's enthusiastic passion for creating and then how he benevolently manages all he has created. In the end, that became more than enough for Job.

Prayers can be informal or formal. Informal prayers are composed of an individual's own words. Whenever prayers are used to provide comfort and to acknowledge the presence of God in a suffering situation, they ought to include references to the sufferer's unique loss(es), circumstances, and grief reactions. These prayers can also include specific requests and petitions for consolation, strength, peace, comfort, hope and healing. And most importantly, prayers should affirm Christ's enduring love and God's abundant compassion. (Eph 3:14-21).

In contrast, formal prayers are established, liturgical prayers that have been shaped by other saints. They can help provide the words when a sufferer or comforter is at a loss for what to pray. As such, formal prayers have the power to create a shared experience with all those who have previously suffered and with all those who are in the midst of suffering. Formal prayers provide witness to other people's adversity and they attest to God's everlasting mercy, grace, and provision. Thus, when formal prayers or other liturgical traditions are used in comforting, they may help to provide insights into the nature of God, his steadfast love and the amazing grace and provision he has shown to others. As a result, formal prayers are mighty avenues to foster hope, consolation and reassurance that our lives are also cradled in his hands.

Formal or common prayers can be located throughout Scripture, in liturgical books such as the Common Prayer Book, The Daily Office, books on prayer, on the Internet, and in the prayers of the ancient church fathers and saints. Some examples of beautiful Scriptural prayers that can be used in the provision of comfort are included in Appendix J.

Prayer is powerful and transformative. Prayer can help to prepare a comforter's heart and mind. Prayer offers the safe spaces for lament, intercession, petitions, confession and repentance, as well as for offering up thanksgiving and praise. They can help a sufferer hear from God, restore and fortify their relationship with him, and provide a deep soul comfort, healing and hope, even in a grinding, winter season.

Lament: Into Thin Air Or…?

Job used lament as an avenue to speak to God and invite him into his adversity, to tell his story, untangle his bewilderment, express the full range of his emotions, and process his grief.

Referencing Job's lament in Chapter 3, Tremper Longman describes laments as being "prayers that are spoken to God when life is falling apart. Laments include complaints about life, other people, oneself and even God."[21] He continues, "the lament often includes an invocation to God and a plea for his help as well as complaints specifying the nature of the problem. Laments might include a confession of sin and a curse against the enemy. Interestingly they almost always end with a note of confidence or even praise of God."[22]

N.T. Wright, in a recent Times magazine article, describes lament as being "what happens when people ask, 'Why?' and don't get an answer."[23] He goes on to state, "the point of lament, woven thus into the fabric of the biblical tradition, is not just that it's an outlet for our frustration, sorrow, loneliness, and sheer inability to understand what is happening or why. The mystery of the biblical story is that *God also laments*. Some Christians like to think of God as above all that, knowing everything, in charge of everything, calm and unaffected by the troubles in his world. That's not the picture we get in the Bible."[24]

In his book, *Prophetic Lament: A Call for Justice in Troubled Times*, Soong-Chan Rah adds to this conversation when he specifically discusses how lament and praise in the grieving process are the two poles which reflect the nature of speaking to God.[25] Rah defines praise as worshiping God and lament as,

> "...prayers of petition arising out of need. But lament is not simply the presentation of complaints, nor merely the expression of sadness over difficult circumstances. Lament in the Bible is a liturgical response to the reality of suffering and engages God in the context of pain and trouble. The hope of lament is that God would respond to human suffering that is wholeheartedly communicated through lament."[26]

Rah asserts that despite the lament's indispensable value in suffering, it is often ignored in the American church.[27] Nathaniel A. Carlson echoes Rah's observation in his article, "Lament: The

Biblical Language of Trauma", when he cites Paul A. Baglyos's comment that the "contemporary American church has become 'so deeply habituated to the absence of lament in their worship that the absence arouses little attention, prompts few objections, and raises few questions.'"28 Carlson goes on to state that "sadly, this neglect of lament isolates trauma survivors (as well as many others who suffer and grieve) from the language they need to both hear and speak in the corporate worship of God's people. In a world of pervasive trauma, the church's exclusion of lament is nothing short of tragic."29

This minimization of lament in the current church is unfortunate because as we witnessed in Job's narrative, lament was a major vehicle for Job to express the full range of his feelings and thoughts, to articulate his grief, and to turn to God and draw him into his suffering experience. It was Job's way to honestly and openly cope with his adversity and with what he perceived to be unfair and unjust treatment. Lament was one of his spiritual response to his overwhelming misfortune and his desperate cry to find God in his suffering.

However, a sufferer can be encouraged to access the ancient laments and liturgical traditions that have been used by the suffering for thousands of years. Carlson contends that the Christian community has been "gifted by God with a wealth of inspired prayers and songs that invites survivors to face God with their traumatic experience."30 Turning to these ancient traditions, Scriptural laments and the words of the saints can be especially helpful when a sufferer needs permission to lament and help to find the words that can fully express all that they are feeling and thinking.

Lament also has the power to heal because it allows a sufferer to air their grievances against God or others and to release the darker emotions and thoughts that they might otherwise repress or ignore. Carlson supports the contention that the lament is more than just a resource that authenticates the human experience because of how it ministers to the suffering and is "uniquely fitted to provide therapeutic benefit."31

Tremper Longman notes that in the beginning stages of his grief Job "is not even addressing his lament to God," but rather it is as though he is "speaking to thin air in his exasperation," "making no innovation or plea for help, nor confessing or protesting his innocence."32 Longman suggests that in this early stage of Job's grief, he is not actually lamenting, but rather he is stuck in complaining, cursing and grumbling.33 Yet, Longman contends that as Job cries out, always in the presence of God, he eventually shifts to lament. He begins to direct his comments towards God, searches for him in his suffering and pleads for his justice and intervention. By the end of the narrative, we see that Job had turned to praise when he acknowledged "I know that you can do all things, and that no purpose of yours can be thwarted" (42:5).

Job's narrative highlights some lasting truths about the importance of lament in suffering. It testifies about the power of lament to process grief and bring healing in suffering. It illustrates how lament can shift a sufferer's focus from complaining and petitions towards anticipation, restoration and a future.

Because of the lament's efficacy and power, comforters are called to create the grace-filled spaces where a sufferer can lament without fear of censure or being criticized. These are the safe spaces that invite complaining, weeping, challenging, cursing, pleading—spaces that absorb the sufferer's conflicted cries that both curse God and praise him, and that invite him into the hard places of suffering so that a sufferer can be moved out of their suffering into hope and restoration.

The Book of Job, Lamentations and the Psalms are extraordinary resources for accessing liturgical laments and accessing ancient wisdom about lament. The laments within these books can be used individually or communally as a way to pray and find comfort.

Reflection and Applications

1. Reflect on the provision of restorative grace in suffering. Consider what stood out to you in the discussion on restorative grace, whether the companions exhibited restorative grace, and the role of grace in unmerited and merited suffering.

2. Reflect on the role of confession and how it helps develop humility and growth in the capacity to offer restorative grace.

3. Have you noticed or experienced someone using Scripture in their attempts to provide comfort? Reflect on how it was received and the degree to which it provided comfort. What things contributed to making it comforting or discomforting? Are there ways it might have been done differently?

4. See Appendix H for an application exercise that offers the opportunity to build a reference list of possible Scripture verses that you could use in suffering and consolation.

5. Reflect on The Book of Job and consider the role prayer played in the support the companions offered Job and how Job used prayer. Reflect on what role, if any, prayer has played when you or others have walked through suffering. Consider how you now might introduce and use prayer to provide comfort.

6. Reflect on lament and its role in suffering and processing grief. Reflect on what your experience in the church has been regarding the teaching and practice of lament. Reflect on how you might use lament in either your own grief or while comforting others.

Chapter Eight
Final Thoughts

"Then Job arose, tore his robe, shaved his head, and fell on the ground and worshipped. He said, 'Naked I came from my mother's womb, and naked shall I return there; the Lord gave, and the Lord has taken away; blessed be the name of the Lord'" (1:20-21).

"But he knows the way that I take; when he has tested me, I shall come out like gold. My foot has held fast to his steps; I have kept his way and have not turned aside. I have not departed from the commandment of his lips; I have treasured in my bosom the words of his mouth" (23:10-12).

"In his hand is the life of every living thing and the breath of every human being" (12:10).

S uffering is uniquely personal *and* a universal human experience.

It is a singular experience in the sense that even when losses may appear to be similar, the way that each of us is impacted by that loss is personal and distinctive.

But it is equally true there are threads in suffering that are common to all humankind. These shared or common threads are woven into the overarching narrative of all human suffering. As Dan B. Allender writes in *The Healing Path*, "none of us escapes the heartache of living in a fallen world. To live is to hurt. We barely take our first breath, and wail is the first sound we utter. Seventy years later (if we're lucky), our exit is with a moan or a whimper, the last breath reminiscent of the first cry."[1]

Yet, we all still struggle when faced with adversity.

It is a painful journey. It is lonely and isolating. It breaks our hearts. It tests the degree of our faith and the strength of our character. It is a path that we would do almost anything to avoid.

Yet, our grief avoidance is one of the things that prevents us from growing in our understanding of suffering, acquiring the skills and the language of grief and stepping into grief in ways that will transform us—the very things that we will need to navigate the next inevitable suffering experience. As Dan Allender aptly points out, "the problem with this position is that once the inevitable pain comes, it is too late to consider how we will allow ourselves to be shaped by it. If we fail to anticipate thoughtfully how we will respond to the harm of living in a fallen world, the pain may be for naught. It will either numb or destroy us rather than refine and even bless us."[2]

I have trudged through a long winter season and can now personally attest to how suffering tests our faith, character, relationships and how we see God in human suffering. My suffering was the very reason that Job's narrative so deeply resonated with me. For a while, I had my own unique journey through loss and grief. It was when I first connected with Job and entered into his experiences that I recognized there were common threads of grief that transcended time, culture and our individual suffering experiences. And when this happened, it became possible to read his narrative and say, "Me too."

Suffering continues to test our beliefs and create paradigm shifts. As Job struggled to fit his experiences into his reward and retribution theology, his belief system was progressively challenged and then gradually reformed. As Longman aptly describes, Job "wrestled with the issue of retribution. He believed that God should reward the righteous and punish the wicked, but his life experience showed the opposite, leading him to question God...But the theology he had been taught (the 'report' of God) was horribly deficient. God did not strictly operate the way Job thought. But now he has had a personal encounter with God, and his understanding is vastly expanded."3

The paradigm shifts in Job's thinking can be evidenced in how Job treated his daughters in the epilogue.

> "He also had seven sons and three daughters. He named the first Jemimah, the second Keziah, and the third Keren-happuch. In all the land there were no women so beautiful as Job's daughters; and their father gave them an inheritance along with their brothers" (42:13-15).

The narrator had revealed in the prologue that Job permitted his first three daughters to attend festivities at their brothers' homes. This signifies that Job granted these daughters a greater degree of freedom than given to most other young daughters in the Ancient Near East. However, these first daughters were never named, nor did they have their own homes or incomes like their brothers. So, it is noteworthy that in the epilogue, these three daughters were named, and Job gave them an inheritance along with their brothers. Carol Meyers, Toni Craven and Ross S. Kraemer, in their commentary, *Women in Scripture: A Dictionary of Named and Unnamed Women in the Hebrew Bible,* highlight the importance of this detail when they assert that "Job undermines patriarchal conventions not only as a name-giver but also in his distribution of property."4 They explain that "according to biblical law (see Numbers 36) only in the absence of male heirs were daughters permitted to receive their father's estate. Here, therefore, is a clear deviation from the law, for Job's daughters inherit alongside their brothers."5

Meyers et al. contend that Job's willingness to defy the biblical law and culture illuminates the degree to which Job's belief systems were transformed through his adversity and meeting God. In his article, "Job, his Daughters and his Wife," Karl G. Wilcox supports this idea when he writes, "Job's ethical reform of his own household means that Job's suffering produced a change in Job's moral perspective that could not have come about if Job had not learned empathy for his daughters as the result of his experience of unjust suffering."6

Job's suffering and hearing from God forced him to grapple with his reward and retribution theology. He learned about God's sovereignty and justice and his passion for creation. He comprehended that God joyfully creates and intentionally cares for every detail of his creation. He grasped that God does not have to answer to humans, nor can he be forced into the neat little boxes of our limited, human reasoning. Job's experiences shifted him from blind and absolute adherence to his theology and moral code, towards a grander vision—one that included a sovereign and mysterious, unpredictable and thrilling God, one who overflows with agape love and restorative grace.

In the epilogue, the narrator writes that "the Lord blessed the latter days of Job more than his beginning" and then describes Job's return to prosperity, listing his vast assets (42:12-16). But we must not conclude that just because God restored Job's prosperity, he will automatically do the same for us. There are no guarantees. God writes a different storyline and conclusion for each of us. Sometimes he will restore what we have lost, but other times he will not. We actually see this evidenced in Job's narrative. Even though the narrator focuses on how Job was doubly blessed after his suffering, we must remember that Job's first ten children were never restored to him and he would never forget his winter season. Some things will remain permanently lost, and some memories will continue to haunt, even if our prosperity returns.

However, it is worth noticing one thing about how the narrator describes Job's prosperity. He seems to be defining prosperity in an earthly, human way. Job's prosperity is discussed in terms of how he now has more camels and sheep and oxen and donkeys and ten more children and lives a long life. But I wonder if Job's return to prosperity can be viewed in another way. Perhaps Job's biggest blessing and his lasting prosperity was not in all the material things, but in his spiritual transformation? Perhaps true prosperity and blessing are the gifts of knowing God, being in an intimate relationship with him, living in restorative grace, knowing that God is for us and with us. And living in the assurance that if we can be like Job and remain faithful through our winter seasons, we too shall come out like gold. These are the gifts beyond measure.

> "But he knows the way that I take; when he has tested me, I shall come out like gold. My foot has held fast to his steps; I have kept his way and have not turned aside. I have not departed from the commandment of his lips; I have treasured in my bosom the words of his mouth" (23:10-12).

Perhaps suffering helps us to understand that our true value is not determined by what we possess, the power we hold, or the status awarded to us in our workplaces and community, but it is defined by the God who created us and who passionately loves us. It is in this truth that we find lasting prosperity.

I have hesitated to share one piece of my suffering narrative because it is very personal, and I feel vulnerable at the mere thought of sharing it. And yet, I recognize that this moment of my narrative was a catalytic moment in my suffering journey. It echoes how Elihu described the way God enters into lives, speaks to his people in a variety of ways, and draws them close.

> "For God speaks in one way, and in two, though people do not perceive it. In a dream, in a vision of the night, when deep sleep falls on mortals, while they slumber on their beds, then he opens their ears, and terrifies them with warnings, that he may turn them aside from their deeds, and keep them from pride, to spare their souls from the Pit, their lives from traversing the River. They are also chastened with pain upon their beds and with continual strife in their bones…Then, if there should be for one of them an angel, a mediator, one of a thousand, one who declares a person upright…God indeed does all these things, twice, three times, with mortals, to bring back their souls from the Pit, so that they may see the light of life" (33:14-30).

I pray that you will gently receive this part of my story in the spirit I offer it. I also pray that it may inspire anyone who wonders about our benevolent Father and where he is in our suffering.

At the lowest point in our time of suffering, every single part of our lives had been impacted by some kind of loss. And although we endured many devastating losses, the losses that were the most crushing for me were the losses that impacted each of our three sons. As a mother, I was heartbroken to watch as all three of them walk through their own adversity. But then, in one particular moment, God broke into my story. I am not sure why he chose this particular moment because there were so many other moments of profound grief that he could have chosen to enter into just as well. But this is reflective of the whole mystery, isn't it?

Our youngest son had always had good health until he diagnosed with Crohn's disease at 21-years-old. Over the next four years, his health experienced a slow, excruciating decline. He lost so much weight that he was almost skeletal. He was weak, unable to carry on a normal life, and had reduced his university studies to part-time. Then late one winter night, as I looked at him lying on the living room couch, I sensed he had slipped into a place that warranted us taking him to the hospital. The specialists had warned us that we would know when he had reached this point. He was reluctant to go because he was worn out and weary. But we insisted. We bundled him up and drove to the emergency room. Because he was so exhausted, he sat in the waiting room while I went to the front desk to sign him in. When the receptionist asked what had brought us there, I burst into tears. She studied me for a moment or two before asking me why I was crying. I replied that I didn't exactly know why. But what I did know, was that I was feeling very afraid and utterly lost. I couldn't quite get my head wrapped around how things had unraveled to the point that his health had become an emergency. The receptionist simply nodded, proceeded to work through the intake form, and then instructed us to wait until they called his name.

The hospital emergency room was abnormally quiet for a Friday night, so he was quickly moved to a bed in the receiving ward. As he waited to see a physician, the nurses ascertained he was dangerously dehydrated. They made the decision to immediately start an IV to get some liquids into him as soon as possible. The nurse tried to insert the IV needle into his forearm, but she was unsuccessful. Dehydration had made his veins difficult to access.

They were so constricted that when she tried to insert the needle, they were collapsing. She tried twice without success. According to protocols, a nurse can only try to insert a needle twice and then must request another nurse to try. So, she called for another nurse to join the people who were now gathered around his bed. I remained off to the side, watching as the second nurse tried to insert the IV needle. She tried twice and was also unsuccessful. My son was experiencing increasing pain after each attempt. The nurses were becoming flustered. I could feel their mounting concern as his treatment was being delayed. They called for a third nurse to try.

I could no longer bear to watch. Leaving my husband to sit with our son, I slipped between the curtains that surrounded his bed and entered the small, open area of the ward. The lights were soft and dim. It was quiet, in the same way an empty school or arena can feel still and tranquil, and yet at the same time feels curiously animated. I felt very alone and very scared.

While I stood motionless, my mind was rushing, spinning through my mental phone directory—seeking, searching for someone I could call. I had a desperate need to talk, to connect with someone, anyone. But every time an image of someone cropped up, I quickly discarded it. It was too late to call them. They would not understand. They were away on holiday. They already had enough troubles and didn't need another one. They'd always seemed rather indifferent to his suffering. In the end, it seemed that there was no one for me to call.

And then, God spoke to me. Gently, calmly, but very distinctly saying, "You can always call on me."

No words can explain or do justice to the way God entered into this space and time, choosing this moment to enter into my personal narrative. I was in that hospital ward, yet suddenly, I was also in that liminal, thin space between heaven and earth, in God's presence. And my response to God's invitation? Undone by his love and grace, I wept. Gave thanks. And called on him.

Over time, I have experienced healing and restoration. Working through my grief has not been a linear process, where I made positive steps towards healing every single day. Rather, my healing has unfolded in a more random fashion, with a few steps forward, followed by a few steps backward, then once again stepping forward. But as time has allowed me to process my grief, I have grown to deeply appreciate all that I learned in my winter season. Suffering journeys can be transformative experiences if we are open to their invitations to learn new things.

Later, as our winter season turned to spring, our disorientation turned to re-orientation, my narrative continued to bear some similarities to Job's narrative. We had lost some people and some things that could never be replaced. There are some relationships that still need prayer and forgiveness and restoration. And like Job, my relationship with God has grown deeper, richer and experiential.

I am now able to accept the mystery of life and the not knowing why life unfolds the way it does. Because I trust that God passionately cares about every single aspect of his creation, I do not have to know everything, control events and rescue everyone.

I have drawn particular comfort from Job's imagery, "In his hand is the life of every living thing, and the breath of every human being" (12:10). Confident that God the Creator formed my beloved and me, gives us breath and life, and lovingly carries us in his capable hands has allowed me to breathe easier about what is around the corner.

Job's narrative showed me how to keep my eyes focused on God—trusting that he has good intentions for me. Waiting on him with what I call patient endurance: the ability to trust God and wait on his timing, even when I am faced with overwhelming adversity and uncertainty.

While Job never learned of the heavenly conversations between Satan and God and his suffering continued to remain a mystery to him, God's speeches gave Job and the reader a glimpse of God's unparalleled glory and majesty that became enough for him. Alongside Job, we glimpse God's unlimited imagination and his unrestrained creativity. We see a vision of God, the passionate and incomparable Creator, who lavishly loves everything that he creates. And as Longman points out, how he especially loves "humanity who occupies a privileged place in God's cosmos."[7]

God's speeches gifted me with a sense of how God is all around us and yet so transcendent and utterly above us. He is eternal and infinite and transcendent and holy. We know God, and yet we can never completely know him.[8] For this reason, St. Augustine wrote, "If you understand, it is not God you understand."[9]

Elihu eloquently spoke about something else that I also discovered in my suffering. In his speech, Elihu exclaimed, "But no one says, 'Where is God my Maker, who gives songs in the night, who teaches us more than the animals of the earth, and makes us wiser than the birds of the air?'" (35:10-11). In his book, *Christian Caregiving*, Hulme picks up on Elihu's phrasing, "*songs of the night,*" when he writes,

> "'Songs in the night' is a biblical metaphor for joy in the midst of trouble. The night hours are the time of fear. Depressed people fear the 4:00 a.m. hour when they awake to their terrors. The subconscious breaks through then into the conscious. The night – and the act of going

to sleep – are also symbols of death and dying. Those who have songs in the night are no longer traumatized by the night. The spiritual person is not one who simply cries out for help when in trouble. Rather, he or she believes also that God can sustain and strengthen in the midst of trouble. It is this expanded insight into God's ways that Elihu sees as the advantage of the believer in times of trouble. The advantage is this capacity of the believer for a different kind of prayer when distressed than the simple cry for help – the capacity for prayer that values and asks for 'songs in the night.' Elihu's description of this advantage of the believer – the covenanted person, the spiritual person – is a prolepsis of what Job will experience in the coming theophany. The night will remain dark, but there will be peace and joy in the midst of it."[10]

Songs in the night. Light in the darkness. Hope in despair. Contentment in chaos. Joy in the midst of trouble. It is hard to believe that we can hold both pain and joy at the same time. But we can, and we do. Joy arrives in our disorientation and winter seasons in extraordinary ways. Often when we least expect it. Even in the moments where the gritty, real-deal stuff of suffering has stripped us down, removed our pride and pretences and positive self-reference. When our eyes are suddenly drawn from our horizontal, earthly heartaches and troubles, vertically towards our Heavenly Father.

And suddenly, spacious places are opened up. Spaces where we meet God, who has been there all along. Waiting for us. He is the Song. And it is he who generously gives us love and compassion, wisdom and inspiration, mercy and grace, provision and protection, and the promise of eternal life. These are the songs in the night that break into our human stories of suffering, even when we are standing in a dimly lit hospital emergency ward, in the middle of a bleak night.

Job's narrative also gives witness to the significance of looking both vertically towards God and horizontally towards caring social connections and community during times of suffering. Through Job's experiences, we learned about the power of social connections and the ability of a companion to either to wound and forsake, or to sustain and comfort. Job's narrative demonstrates how adversity can be intensified when a comforter walks into suffering with agendas, bias, a closed mind. Consolation becomes miserable, the comforter a worthless physician. In contrast, I pray that we've learned how to lean into suffering in ways that respect the sufferer and honor the individual nature of their suffering journey.

In one of my seminary classes that focused on loss, suffering and dying, the professor, Dr. Gloria Woodland, spoke about the rights of a mourner and distributed a handout entitled the *Mourner's Bill of Rights,* written by Dr. Alan D. Wolfelt. I have included a copy of it in Appendix L. The value in knowing the rights of a sufferer is that it helps us to form boundaries and guidelines for suffering experiences. It helps everyone to be clear about what is reasonable behavior to expect and what are compassionate ways to treat others in adversity. When I first saw a copy of the *Mourner's Bill of Rights,* I immediately thought about Job in his adversity. I imagined how things might have been different for him had they all been aware of these rights. Perhaps these guidelines would have guided the companions to become more consoling comforters. Likewise, I wondered how the guidelines might have helped Job to know what was reasonable to expect from his companions. But regardless, the reality is that having some guidelines regarding the rights of a sufferer can make a positive difference in the provision of comfort.

As we are ending, it is important to mention that just as there are seasons of suffering, there will also be seasons that are better than others for a comforter to enter into someone else's suffering. It is critical that comforters are self-aware and sensitive about where they are at emotionally, spiritually and physically. Whenever a comforter is in the midst of their own suffering or feeling burned out, emotional, fragile, fatigued, empty or overwhelmed, they should not take on more suffering and pain. These are the times that a comforter should focus on their own self-care, healing and well-being.

While I was in my winter season and then afterward, as I was processing my grief, I temporarily stepped away from counselling and doing ministry. I recognized that I was not in a healthy enough place to absorb more suffering and provide consolation to others. But as I have moved through and past my grieving, I am now feeling ready to once again reach out and comfort others.

Job's narrative affirms another important truth. God is steadfast, trustworthy and compassionate through every season of life, in both merited and unmerited suffering. Longman writes that God "neither destroys nor abandons sinful humanity but pursues their redemption in a way that leads to the cross of Christ."[11] Longman further suggests that while God permitted Job to suffer, he did not "let Job continue on a path that might lead to his destruction," intervening in a timely manner "so that Job maintain[ed] a healthy relationship with his Maker."[12] What a wonderful reminder that our God, who is full of grace, is in the restoration and redemption business.[13]

There is no doubt that suffering has the power to transform us. But it is important to note that it is not the suffering per se that transforms us, but rather how we choose to enter into and walk through our grief. As I stumbled through our winter season, I saw this specific truth play out over and over again. Everyone who was part of my narrative of suffering or touched by it grieved differently, according to their own timetable, agenda, and ability. And in the end, because of the way each individual chose to deal with their grief, some were transformed through their suffering, some remained stuck, and some grew hard hearted.

As we shared in Job's experience, we were brought face to face with a God who surpasses what mere mortal minds can possibly fathom. As a result, both Job and the reader are confronted with a decision. Are we willing to accept the mystery of God? His role in human suffering? And serve the just God who does know why there is suffering in the world? Will we be like Job and accept God's sovereignty and trust that his divine plans are to prosper us and all humankind?

In the end, we saw that Job decided that knowing God was enough. God was the answer. And so, he submitted himself into God's loving care, his providential timing, provision and protection. The question remains for each one of us: what will we decide?

Let us retain hope and optimism and joy as we begin to face and step into the hard spaces of suffering, and as we reach out to comfort each other. For a while, we will misstep and slip-up, and we may resemble the miserable comforters far more than we would like, we can rest in the assurance that as we remain open to learning, abide in Christ, and let the Holy Spirit empower us, we will be transformed into consoling comforters.

As we draw on the insights gleaned from Job's narrative and others' and our own suffering and embody them in our own lives, we will make a positive difference for others. And as we participate in God's eternal narrative, we will be transformed in our capacity to love others, offer restorative grace and will navigate suffering in ways that glorify our Heavenly Father.

So, as we finish, I invite you to rise and respond to Teresa of Avila's familiar words of encouragement that echo across the centuries,

"Christ has no body now, but yours. No hands, no feet on earth, but yours. Yours are the eyes through which Christ looks compassion into the world. Yours are the feet with which Christ walks to do good. Yours are the hands with which Christ blesses the world" (1515-1582).

In closing,

May you feel God's abiding presence throughout all seasons.

May you know God is nearby, even when he remains silent.

May you remain certain of God's agape love, amazing grace, and good intentions for you, even as you face trials and walk through suffering.

May you experience the mystery and the wonder of the Creator and his Creation.

May you hear songs in the night.

May you experience consolation and become willing to offer consolation.

And may you rest in the assurance that God is always available, always inviting you, to call on him anytime.

In his presence,

Anne

Final Reflections

1. Reflect on which aspects of Job's narrative that most resonate with you. Reflect on the similarities and differences between his suffering experiences and yours.

2. What were some insights for you regarding how loss and grief can lead to our transformation?

3. One of Job's main struggles was trying to find God in his suffering. Yet, throughout his grief, he remained faithful and passed the tests that Satan put him through. Reflect on how you have been tested in your life, how the experience(s) of suffering shifted your faith and belief systems, and how you experienced God in your suffering.

4. Reflect back through the book and consider which topics, themes or skills that most deeply impacted or resonated with you. Reflect on what you have learned; what you will take away from this study and will now use in your own suffering and as you provide consolation.

5. After reading this book, reflect on how you are now feeling about entering into someone else's suffering. What might you do differently and what might you still need to focus on so that you become more willing and able to walk through your own or others' suffering?

6. The Book of Job focuses primarily on Job's unmerited suffering and God's place in innocent suffering. In contrast, the Book of Lamentations focuses primarily on the disobedience and merited suffering of the Israelites, and the resultant destruction of Jerusalem and the temple. Lamentations covers the misery and laments of the entire community as they walk through merited suffering due to their sinful behavior and God's just response.

Perhaps the Book of Lamentations is a worthy follow-up to this conversation around the Book of Job and unmerited suffering. It may be helpful to learn what Lamentations can teach us about suffering.

7. As we conclude, are there thoughts or notions or biases that have shifted as you moved through this book? Are you noticing and paying attention to your thoughts and feelings as we end?

<u>Appendix A</u>. Brief Summary Of The Book Of Job

The Prologue, Chapters 1 and 2. Conversations Between God and Satan

- Describes how Job, a prosperous and righteous man, suddenly experienced one misfortune after another. He lost everything: all his possessions, his entire estate, his ten children, and eventually, his health when he was inflicted by a debilitating disease.

- Job suffered a wide range of grief reactions: financially when he lost his entire estate, emotionally when all 10 of his children died (1:18-19), socially when he lost his reputation and standing in the community and became isolated (Ch. 2), physically when he suffered open sores and discomfort, and spiritually when he searched for meaning and for God, and struggled to understand why a good God was allowing him to suffer.

- "Now when Job's three friends heard of all these troubles that had come upon him, each of them sets out from his home - Eliphaz the Temanite, Bildad the Shuhite, and Zophar the Naamathite. They met together to go and console and comfort him" (2:11).

- Initially, they commiserated with Job in a supportive and positive manner. They "raised their voices and wept aloud; they tore their robes and threw dust in the air upon their heads. They sat with him on the ground seven days and seven nights, and no one spoke a word to him, for they saw that his suffering was very great" (2:11-13).

- The companions sought to support Job by being physically present, providing companionship, and engaging in traditional grieving practices.

Chapters 3 to 37: Conversations Between Job and his Companions

- The companions' support quickly moved from being consoling into an accusatory and critical series of speeches, leading to heated debates about the meaning and reasons for why Job was suffering and how he could move forward and regain his prosperity.

- The key thread running through the speeches revolved around the question, "Why?" Why had God allowed such a righteous man like Job to experience such tragedy? Job's companions believed the answer was found in their reward and retribution theology—that Job's suffering had been caused by his sin.

- Job's companions used theological arguments and referenced Scripture (Torah) to defend their stance. They held the fundamental belief that because God is just, he would never allow an innocent person to suffer, only those who had sinned. Therefore, the only explanation they had for the tragedy that had befallen Job is that he must have sinned (34:12). Their arguments were rooted in their theology that the greater the trials, the greater the sins that person must have committed (4:7-8; 8:6-8; 10-13).

Appendix

- Job is confused because he knew he was innocent. He observed that the wicked thrive (24:22-23) and the innocent suffered. His theology of God's justice, that he rewards the righteous and punished the wicked, no longer made sense because it no longer fit with his experience and what he observed going on around him. In his confusion and anguish he lamented, cried out, accused, protested and questioned God. He demanded to know and understand what has happened to him. He desperately wanted to understand why he, a righteous man, had to suffer (7:20; 16:18-21; 23:9)

- Job's companions insisted that if Job confessed his sins and repented, then God would deliver him from his pain and restore his fortune (5:17-26; 11:15; 22:25).

- Job refused to accept their interpretation of why he was suffering. He was unable to fathom that he or any other innocent sufferer should assume full responsibility for their suffering. He believed that God had the answers.

- Job challenged his friends and called them "miserable comforters" (16:2) and "worthless physicians" (13:4). He suggested that it would be better if they refrained from their hurtful, minimizing, critical, and disregarding comments and simply "keep silent" because their behavior was compounding his suffering (13:5).

Chapters 38-42:6: God/Yahweh Speaks with Job

- After Job and his companions engaged in lengthy debate, God finally appeared and addressed Job.

179

- God did not provide the answers Job was seeking. God never addressed the mystery around Job's suffering. He did not answer Job or the companions' questions about why God allows suffering. He never resolved the issues around the justice or injustice of Job's tribulations.

- Instead, God illuminated his love of creating, his delight in all that he creates, how he alone governs the universe and humans' inability to grasp the intricacies and mystery of his creation and plans (Ch. 38-41). While there were no concrete or specific answers to all Job's questions, in the end Job discovered that God is the answer. And trusting in him was enough.

Epilogue, 42:7-17: Job's Transformation

- God then rebuked the companions for not speaking rightly about him, as his servant Job has done. He commands the companions to make a sacrifice and for Job to pray for them. He declared he will accept Job's prayers for them rather than deal with them according to their folly. The companions and Job obeyed and follow God's instructions.

- After Job had prayed for his companions, God restored Job's fortunes and gave him twice as much as he had before.

- The community who had known him before, came to Job and they feasted together and ate bread, they showed him sympathy and comforted him for all the evil that the Lord had brought upon him and each gave him money and a gold ring.

Appendix

- The Lord blessed Job more in the second half of his life than in his first, blessing him with the return of his estate, wealth, seven sons and three daughters, whom he named Jemimah, Keziah, and Keren-happuch. The daughters were the most beautiful women in all the land and Job gave them an inheritance along with their brothers.

- Job lived a long life and was able to see his children and his children's children, and died when he was old and full of days.

<u>Appendix B</u>: List Of Feeling Words

Examples of Pleasant Feelings

Happy	Good	Caring	Playful	Open	Attraction/ Engaging
Delighted	Thankful	Loving	Energetic	Inviting	Interested
Thrilled	Calm	Thoughtful	Happy	Comfortable	Intrigued
Overjoyed	Encouraged	Kind	Free	Confident	Attracted
Elated	Peaceful	Gentle	Alive	Welcoming	Frisky
Joyous	Contented	Devoted	Curious	Optimistic	Admiration
Gleeful	Satisfied	Passionate	Inquisitive	Brave	Touched
Blessed	Secure	Tender	Wondering	Courageous	Impacted
Encouraged	Productive	Considerate	Creative	Liberated	Attentive
Relaxed	Bold	Giving	Eager	Inquisitive	Attached
Glad	Confident	Supportive	Inventive	Friendly	Engaged
Pleased	Inspired	Nurturing	Silly	Inspired	Fascinated
Cheerful	Gratified	Helpful	Cheerful	Trusting	Focused
Excited	Serene	Compassionate	Spontaneous	Warm-hearted	Determined
Animated	Appreciative	Attentive	Whimsical	Thoughtful	Inspired
Ecstatic	Comfortable	Friendly	Imaginative	Respectful	Involved
Euphoric	Satisfied	Understanding	Lively	Tolerant	Ambitious
Buoyant	Safe	Consoling	Spirited	Yielding	Absorbed
Jovial	Secure	Nurturing	Amused	Receptive	Desirous
Merry	Assured	Giving	Liberated	Genial	Passionate
Jubilant	Mellow	Connected	Excited	Accepting	Motivated
Festive	Relaxed	Attached	Exhilarated	Understanding	Devoted
Pleased	Tranquil	Affectionate	Zippy	Earnest	Aroused
Fulfilled	Serene	Cherishing	Vibrant	Soft	Enthralled
Expectant	Aglow	Ardent	Jovial	Adaptable	Keen
Optimistic	Empowered	Thoughtful	Sparkling	Agreeable	Cherishing
Blissful	Rejuvenated	Comforted	Amazed	Amiable	Admiring
Satisfied	Rested	Empathetic	Astonished	Benevolent	Appreciative
Certainty	Refreshed	Encouraging	Adventurous	Secure	Fervent
Hopeful	Centered	Responsive	Fascinated	Relaxed	Infatuated
Euphoric	Mellow		Animated		Daring
			Exuberant		Admiring
			Amused		

Appendix

Examples of Unpleasant Feelings

Grief/Sadness	Anger	Inadequacy	Confusion	Hurt	Fear
Sorrow	Mad	Underconfident	Unbelieving	Vulnerable	Fearful
Pained	Furious	Unsure	Confounded	Broken	Terrified
Heartbroken	Annoyed	Damaged	Bewildered	Wounded	Scared
Devasted	Outraged	Impotent	Conflicted	Insulted	Timid
Overwhelmed	Indignant	Inferior	Torn	Disrespected	Anxious
Empty	Frustrated	Powerless	Uncertain	Violated	Uncertain
Immobilized	Aggressive	Useless	Wondering	Betrayed	Paralyzed
Shocked	Pissed off	Washed up	Confused	Abused	Vulnerable
Gloomy	Fuming	Feeble	Puzzled	Pained	Apprehensive
Adrift	Inflexible	Deficient	Fuzzy	Burdened	Jittery
Barren	Impatient	Incomplete	Moody	Fatigued	Inhibited
Bleak	Belligerent	Ineffective	Baffled	Forgotten	Bashful
Despondent	Bitter	Incapable	Befuddled	Empty	Unsure
Desolate	Enraged	Helpless	Flustered	Devalued	Worried
Dejected	Incensed	Inept	Disconcerted	Isolated	Alarmed
Crestfallen	Infuriated	Overwhelmed	Disorganized	Forsaken	Desperate
Grieved	Seething	Weak	Disquieted	Abandoned	Distressed
Distressed	Provoked	Broken	Taken-aback	Deceived	Horrified
Dispirited	Vengeful	Inept	Stunned	Lonely	Paralyzed
Lost	Vindictive	Struggling	Stumped	Destroyed	Nervous
Melancholy	Unforgiving	Flawed	Disturbed	Demoralized	Shaky
Miserable	Aggravated	Inferior	Foggy	Rejected	Skittish
Downcast	Annoyed	Whipped	Misunderstood	Minimized	Threatened
Regretful	Bothered	Exhausted	Mixed up	Excluded	Cautious
Weepy	Resentful	Defeated	Undecided	Ridiculed	Uneasy
Morose	Spiteful	Ailing	Unsettled	Disappointed	Unsure
Sorry	Ticked off	Imperfect	Unsure	Devastated	Watchful
Downhearted	Irritated	Incapable	Distracted	Discredited	Timid
Remorseful	Testy	Insignificant	Rattled	Maligned	Tense
Crestfallen	Sullen	Lacking	Thrown	Mistreated	Jumpy
Repentant	Impatient	Dry	Adrift	Resentful	Fretful
Contrite	Dismayed	Apathetic	Ambivalent	Troubled	Afraid
Empty	Hostile	Burned out	Astonished	Neglected	Panicked
Anguish	Bugged	Tired	Undecided	Aching	Intimidated
Bereft	Chagrined	Exhausted	Doubting	Shamed	Petrified
Crushed	Irked	Discouraged	Mystified	Wronged	Careful
Desolate	Irate	Disheartened	Perplexed	Judged	Tentative
Despairing	Grouchy	Fatigued	Preoccupied	Criticized	Agitated
Devastated	Truculent	Listless	Spaced out	Debased	Alarmed
Gloomy	Argumentative	Powerless	Unbelieving	Humiliated	Dread
Morose	Hostile	Trapped	Weird	Alienated	Hesitant
Worked-up	Defensive	Weary	Wishy-washy	Ambushed	Insecure
Wretched	Seething		Disillusioned	Ignored	

Appendix C: Feeling Faces

HOW DO I FEEL RIGHT NOW?

* **Although there are many wonderful resources for adults to access regarding how to help a child who is suffering, here are two examples of the possible resources that are available:**

Kroen, William C. *Helping Children Cope With the Loss of a Loved One: A Guide for Grownups*, Minneapolis, MN: free spirit Publishing, 1996.

Mellonie, Bryan and Ingpen, Robert. *Lifetimes: the beautiful way to explain death to children*, Toronto: Bantam Books, 1993.

<u>Appendix D</u>: The Tangled Emotions In Grief

Appendix E: Empathetic, Reflective Responses.

Part 1: Application: Empathetic Responses.

Imagine that you are one of Job's companions. You are sitting with him on the ash heap, listening to him as he grieves. You are observing Job carefully, noticing what his non-verbal behavior is revealing, listening to what he is saying and what his words are implying. You are being attentive to Job so that you can more fully appreciate and grasp what he is thinking and feeling. The better your focus on Job, the more likely you will be able to provide him healing consolation.

The following exercise instructs you to turn to specific Scripture verses where Job is speaking and reacting to his losses.

As you read each Scripture verse, spend time carefully listening to Job, reflecting on what he is feeling and attempting to verbalize.

Use the list of feeling words in the chart in Appendix B to help you identify and label his feelings.

Once you have identified what you think Job is feeling, use one of the following empathetic phrases suggested below to create an empathetic, consoling response.

Examples of possible empathetic responses:

- o "It seems like you are feeling _____ and _____ right now."
- o "I'm hearing that you are _____ by all that has happened."

- "Since your loss, it sounds like it has been hard for you to _____."
- "Losing _____ has contributed to your feeling _____."
- "You're feeling _____."
- "It sounds like you are feeling _____."
- "You're really _____."
- "As I was listening to you, I sensed that you are feeling _____ about _____."
- "It seems you thinking about your loss and these thoughts are making you feel _____."
- "I am getting the sense that you are_____."

Scripture Verse:	What emotion(s) do you think Job is feeling and trying to express in this verse?	What is an empathetic response that acknowledges what Job is trying to communicate about his feelings?
Job 16:2	e.g. angry, exasperated, offended, harassed, frustrated, misunderstood	e.g. "Job, it sounds like you are feeling offended and frustrated by your companions' comments."
Job 16:10		
Job 19:25-27		
Job 14:7-12		
Job 30:30-31		e.g. "You seem to be in such pain. It sounds like you are physically and emotionally exhausted."
Job 42:3-6	e.g. self-deprecating, chastened, sheepish, apologetic, remorseful	e.g. "I am hearing that you regret you spoke about things you did not fully understand."

Part 2: Application: Empathetic Responses

Read the following Scripture verses listed in the chart below that focus on Job's physical grief reactions. Then complete the chart by listing the physical reaction(s) observed, any response that was made by the miserable comforters to that reaction, and in the third column, create an empathetic response that a consoling comforter could make in relation to Job's physical reactions. Reference the empathetic phrasing learned in the last session.

Physical Reactions:	Scripture Verse: Job	Miserable Comforters' Response(s):	Possible Consoling Comforters' Response(s):
His changed appearance.	*2:12*	*e.g. they wailed, ripped their clothing, sprinkled dust on their heads*	*e.g. Cry with them. Gently hug them. Possible responses: "I sense you are in such discomfort." or "You must be in such agony."*
Sleep disturbances, can't find rest	*3:26; 7:3-4; 30:17*		
Food is tasteless, has no desire to eat, thought of food makes Job feel ill	*6:7*		*e.g. "Food is so unappealing to you right now that it makes you feel sick even thinking about it."*

Skin is blackened, broken, hardened, and festering	*7:5; 30:30*		e.g. *"I can't help but notice your skin. It looks so painful..."*
Relentless pain	*16:6-7; 30:17*		
Weight loss	*16:8; 17:7; 19:20*		e.g. *"You mentioned feeling shriveled up. I wonder if this is something you feel both physically and emotionally – like there is nothing of you left..."*
Mentions slashed kidneys and gall spilling on the ground	*16:13*		
Red face from crying, shadows under his eyes	*16:16*		

Mentions fever	*30:30*		*"You mention you are feeling feverish... Just one more thing to bear..." "What else might we do to help get your fever down?"*
Mentions loss of strength	*16:15; 17:7*		

<u>Appendix F</u>: Open-Ended Questions

Part 1: Application: Open and Closed-Ended Questions

The following exercise focuses on some of the questions the miserable comforters asked Job. The goal of this exercise is to help solidify an understanding of the difference between a closed-ended and open-ended question. As you read and reflect on each Scripture verse below, consider whether the question meets the criteria for being a closed-ended or open-ended question. Record your reflections in the spaces provided.

Note: The Message translation was used for these exercises because its contemporary language may help to make the companions' questions and the narrator's comments easier to understand.

Miserable Comforters' Questions:	Closed or open-ended question?
E.g. "If you were truly wise, would you sound so much like a windbag, belching hot air?" (15:2)	*Closed-ended*
"Why do you let your emotions take over, lashing out and spitting fire..." (15:12)	
"So what if you were righteous—would God Almighty even notice? Even if you gave a perfect performance, do you think he'd applaud?" (22:3)	
"Where in the world did you learn all this? How did you become so inspired?" (26:4)	
"Think! Has a truly innocent person ever ended up on the scrap heap?" (4:7)	
"Does God mess up? Does God Almighty ever get things	

backward?" (8:3)	
"What do you know that we don't know? What insights do you have that we've missed?" (15:9)	
"What a flood of words! Shouldn't we put a stop to it? Should this kind of loose talk be permitted?" (11:1)	

Part 2: Application: Open-Ended and Closed-Ended Questions

This exercise continues to focus on how a closed-ended question differs from an open-ended question. Read the following Scripture verses and then, in the spaces provided after these closed ended questions, provide two examples of how they could be altered to become more effective open-ended questions. Remember to start your questions with "what," "how," "when," "where," "who" and occasionally "why."

Scripture Passages, Closed-Ended Questions:	Possible Open-Ended Question:	Possible Open-Ended Question:
E.g. "Do you think it's because he cares about your purity that he's disciplining you, putting you on the spot?" (22:4)	*"What are some reasons that might explain why God has allowed you to suffer such losses?"*	*"How are you feeling about the sense that God is rebuking you and bringing charges against you?"*
"But shouldn't your devout life give you confidence now?" (4:6)		
"How can mere mortals be more		

righteous than God?" (4:17)		
"Do you think you can explain the mystery of God?" (11:7)	*"How might you explain the mystery around God?"*	
"Are God's promises not enough for you, spoken so gently and tenderly?" (15:11)		
"Are any of us strong enough to give God a hand or smart enough to give him advice?" (22:2)	*"What are some ways you think man can work with God?"*	
"Do you want the world redesigned to suit you?" (18:4)		

Part 3: Application: Open-Ended Questions

Oftentimes, the comforter can also ask open-ended questions about something that they have noticed in the sufferer's non-verbal behavior or that sufferer has just hinted at or alluded to.

These questions draw attention to the messages that the sufferer has communicated non-verbally through their physical behavior, the tone, speed, and volume of their speech, their difficulty in articulating words, or through other non-verbal behaviors such as clenching their jaws, slumped shoulders, wringing their hands, crying, not making eye contact, or pacing.

In the following exercise, consider each of the Scripture passages and determine what might be being communicated about Job's emotional, cognitive or spiritual reactions through his non-verbal behavior, actions or words.

Then in the spaces provided, create open-ended questions that could have been posed which would have acknowledged Job's reactions and which could have encouraged Job to reflect on what had been noticed.

Appendix

Scripture Verse:	Example of an Open-Ended Question:	Create Your Own Open-Ended Question:
"Satan left God and struck Job with terrible sores. Job was ulcers and scabs from head to foot. They itched and oozed so badly that he took a piece of broken pottery to scrape himself, then went and sat on a trash heap, among the ashes" (2:7-8).	*"Job, I noticed you scratching your sores. They must be unbearably itchy and you must be in such discomfort. What have you already tried to ease the irritation? What else might we try to relieve the pain?"*	
"When they first caught sight of him, they couldn't believe what they saw...!" (2:12)	*"You are suffering. What might we do to help care for you and help relieve some of your pain?"*	
"Do you think I can pull myself up by my bootstraps? Why, I don't even have any boots!" (6:13)	*"It sounds like you feel stuck. What things might you try to regain your footing?"*	
"I hate this life! Who needs any more of this? Let me alone! There's nothing to my life—it's nothing but smoke" (7:15-16) .	*"It sounds like things are so hard that you hate your life right now and want to be left alone. What can we do to help?"*	

<u>Appendix G</u>: Application: Simple Observations And Sharing our Story

Take some time to compose one or two stories about your loss experiences, using the four to five-sentence format suggested below. This format is just a guide to help you compose a few short observations about some aspect of your loss experience(s). Taking the time to compose a short observation(s) and then practice saying them out loud a number of times, will help to ensure that when you are providing comfort, you will be prepared to make an observation about your experiences in a timely, concise, appropriate, and supportive way.

Use this simple frame to help you compose a longer observation that focuses on your personal experience:

- o Start with one introductory statement which clarifies that while it is impossible to know exactly what they are going through, because their narrative is unique, we have also walked a path of loss and grief.

- o A second statement that briefly mentions the type of loss(es).

- o A third statement that mentions where we too struggled to find our way through the grief and,

- o a final statement or two which summarizes how God comforted us, met us and worked within that loss and helped to sustain us.

<u>Appendix H</u>: When Another Is Needed: A List of Possible Non-Emergency and Emergency Referrals:

Non-Emergency Referrals

The following is a brief sampling of some of the many resources available for a sufferer when someone else is needed:

o The Internet provides lists of local and qualified professionals such as lawyers, financial advisors, funeral directors, or loss and grief support groups.

o The local *Hospice.*

o *Canadian Mental Health* (https://cmha.ca/mental-health/finding-help),

o *Mental and Behavioral Health* (https://www.healthlinkbc.ca/health-topics/center1028)

o *Mental Health* (phone 8-1-1, any time of the day, any day of the year).

o *Parents Help Line* (1-855-427-2736).

o *Kids Help Phone* (1-800-668-6868).

o The local *hospital emergency* or reaching their *medical doctor* or *health care provider.*

o *Alcohol & Drug Information and Referral Service* (1-800-663-1441) o Going to the provincial or state registry of *registered counsellors and psychologists*. For example, *British Columbia Association of Registered Clinical Counsellors* website (https://bc-counsellors.org/) which has a list of possible counsellors and their areas of expertise. They can also recommend a counsellor or how to locate possible resources.

o Contacting their *church* and connecting with their *pastor* or the pastor of the Care and Compassion ministry.

o Contacting their *counsellor at their high school or university.*

o Contacting the *RCMP or Police non-emergency line.*

o Contacting the 24/7 *Nurse Hotline* or 811, HealthLine, BC.

o Many companies also have an *Employee Assistance Plan* (EAP). These are a plan that the employee pays into, which they can access for confidential and free counselling with qualified, registered counsellors. Usually, a human resource director or the union representative will know if that company has an EAP. Also, the contract an employee signs usually will state if there is a company EAP.

o *Gambling Anonymous Hotline* (1-855-222-5542)

o *Transition Houses and Safe Homes (1-800-563-0808 or* https://www.bchousing.org/housing-assistance/women-fleeing-violence/transition-houses-safe-homes

Some Possible Emergency Referrals:

There may be occasions where the comforter senses that the sufferer is in a crisis situation. Something about the sufferer's behavior or speech and actions is suggesting that they may be thinking about hurting themselves or hurting someone else.

Sometimes they will just hint at something they are feeling or thinking about, and at other times, they will be quite explicit about what they are thinking.

Norman Wright states that if a comforter is confused by what a sufferer has shared, they should not hesitate to ask for clarification.* It is important to note that in these situations it is *not* the comforter's responsibility to make a formal assessment or to provide the on-going, major support, but it is a comforter's responsibility to ask some simple clarifying questions to get a sense of the risk of self-harm or danger to someone else, and then make sure that the sufferer is linked to the proper supports and resources.

Some examples of simple clarifying questions or statements might be,

- o "You just said _____. Tell me more about that...."
- o "You mentioned you are feeling so down, it might just be better to end it all. I am concerned about you and want you to help me understand what you mean by ending it all."
- o "I hear you say it is so bad that you're thinking of hurting yourself. Please tell me more about that...How are you thinking of hurting yourself?"
- o "When you say you would like to go over there right now and give it to them, what exactly are you thinking?"

In any higher-risk situation, the comforter must suggest that the sufferer connect with an appropriate professional/phone hotline support etc.

Possible Emergency Referrals:

- o Family physician.

- The *24-Hour Crisis and Suicide Prevention Line* (British Columbia: 1-604-872-3311 or Canadian: 1-833-456-4566: TEXT: 45645) These are great resources in a crisis. For twenty-four hours a day, these services have volunteers who are trained to provide crisis support and know the local resources that are available to provide support. They are also trained to answer questions and provide direction when someone is concerned, but uncertain how to handle a situation.

- The *24-hour Women's Support Line* (604-987-3374)

- *Mental Health Helpline:* (phone 8-1-1, any time of the day, any day of the year).

- The *police or RCMP non-emergency or emergency number.*

- Going directly to the *emergency room at a hospital.*

- *Contacting their guardian*(s) if they are underage.

- *Crisis Grief and Loss. Bereavement Helplines* (1-877-779-2223, or https://crisiscentre.bc.ca/community-services/grief-and-loss/

* Norman Wright, *Helping Those Who Hurt,* p. 104.

<u>Appendix I</u>: Showing up, Acts Of Service

Read Romans 12:9-21, entitled *"Love in Action"* and reflect on what this passage teaches about acts of service. While this is a passage from the New Testament, its principles about being love in action can be applied to help us understand the support Job did or did not receive. Reflect on whether the companions exhibited the love in action concepts discussed in this passage as they tried to comfort Job.

<u>Appendix J</u>: Examples Of Scriptural Prayers That Can Be Used In Suffering

Prayer:	Scripture Reference:
Job's Prayer of Confession and Repentance	Job 42:1-6
The Lord's Prayer	Matthew 6:9-13
Jonah's Prayer for Salvation	Jonah 2:2-9
David's Prayer for Deliverance	Psalm 3
Hannah's Prayer of Praise	1 Samuel 2:1-10
Prayer Relating to God's Love in Suffering	Romans 5:1-11
Prayer Relating to Eternal Life	2 Corinthians 4:16-5:1-10
Moses Prayer for Israel While in the Wilderness	Exodus 32:9-14
David's Prayer for Pardon and Confession of Sin	Psalm 51
Mariam's Song of Praise for Deliverance	Exodus 15:20-21
David's Psalm of Surrender	Psalm 139
Nehemiah's Prayer for Success	Nehemiah 1:4-11
Jesus's Prayer of Submission at Gethsemane	Luke 22:39-46
Paul's Prayer for the Ephesian	Ephesians 1:15-23

Appendix

Believers	
Prayer of a Sufferer	Psalm 102
Prayer of Jabez	1 Chronicles 4:10
Hezekiah's Petitions for Deliverance and Healing	2 Kings 19:14-19; 20:1-7
Daniel's Confession on Behalf of His People	Daniel 9:4-19

<u>Appendix K</u>: Application, Building A Scripture Resource.

The goal of this exercise is to establish a list of verses that relate to some of the common themes that inevitably crop up in suffering. When completed, the list could be photocopied and tucked into a Bible, a wallet or purse so that you can quickly reference it when you are in the midst of grieving or consolation.

To get you started, this list provides just a sampling of the many Scripture passages that might be consoling in grief. Spaces have been left for you to add verses that particularly resonate with you.

To continue building this list, you might re-read Job, read Ecclesiastes, Proverbs, Lamentations and the Psalms, look at the Subject Index in your Bible or refer to a Bible Commentary or research the Internet, so that you can find additional verses.

Consider this as an on-going activity where you can continue to add relevant verses as you come across them.

Theme:	Old Testament Verses:	New Testament Verses:
God is Sovereign.	Job 1:21; 9:11, 9:19, Job 12:10, 12:13, 21:22, 42:2 Proverbs 16:9 Isaiah 55:8-9	Ephesians 1:11
God is love.	Nehemiah 9:17 Isaiah 54:10	I John 4:7-12 John 3:16

God is faithful.	Deuteronomy 7:9 Psalm 119:90 Lamentations 3:30-33	1 Thessalonians 5:24 Revelation 19:11
God is good and has good intentions. **(heals, refines, redeems transforms)**	Job 5:17-18, 7:17, 23:10, 42:2-6 Psalms 119:71 Nahum 1:7	2 Corinthians 1:3-6 Philippians 1:6 James 5:10-11
God protects and provides.	Job 10:12, 33:4, 38:41 Joshua 1:9 Habakkuk 3:17-19 Psalm 34:17-22	Matthew 11:28 Philippians 4:11-13, 4:19
God provides peace and hope.	Job 5:9-11, 9:10, 11:13-19 Deuteronomy 31:8	Romans 15:4
God invites prayers and laments.	Jeremiah 33:3 Deuteronomy 31:8-9	Ephesians 6:18

God is trustworthy.	Job 19:25-27; 34:14-20 Psalm 67 Isaiah 42:3	Hebrews 13:5 Romans 8:28
Laments.	The Book of Job and Lamentations Psalm 3, 6, 13, 25:16-20; 42:4-7; 102:1-2	Mark 5:38; Luke 8:52: Matthew 2:18
Eternal Life.	Job 14:7	Revelations 21:4-5 1 John 5:11 John 3:16-17
God understands suffering.	Isaiah 53:3-12 Psalm 139:3	John 11:35 Matthew 26:36-39

<u>Appendix L.</u> Mourner's Bill Of Rights

By Alan D. Wolfelt, Ph.D.

Though you should reach out to others as you do the work of mourning, you should not feel obligated to accept the unhelpful responses you may receive from some people.

You are the one who is grieving, and as such, you have certain "rights" no one should try to take away from you.

The following list is intended both to empower you to heal and to decide how others can and cannot help. This is not to discourage you from reaching out to others for help, but rather to assist you in distinguishing useful responses from hurtful ones.

1. You have the right to experience your own unique grief. No one else will grieve in exactly the same way you do. So, when you turn to others for help, don't allow them to tell what you should or should not be feeling.

2. You have the right to talk about your grief.

Talking about your grief will help you heal. Seek out others who will allow you to talk as much as you want, as often as you want, about your grief. If at times you don't feel like talking, you also have the right to be silent.

3. You have the right to feel a multitude of emotions.

Confusion, disorientation, fear, guilt and relief are just a few of the emotions you might feel as part of your grief journey. Others may try to tell you that feeling angry, for example, is wrong. Don't take these judgmental responses to heart. Instead, find listeners who will accept your feelings without condition.

4. You have the right to be tolerant of your physical and emotional limits. Your feelings of loss and sadness will probably leave you feeling fatigued. Respect what your body and mind are telling you. Get daily rest. Eat balanced meals. And don't allow others to push you into doing things you don't feel ready to do.

5. You have the right to experience "griefbursts."

Sometimes, out of nowhere, a powerful surge of grief may overcome you. This can be frightening, but is normal and natural. Find someone who understands and will let you talk it out.

6. You have the right to make use of ritual.

The funeral ritual does more than acknowledge the death of someone loved. It helps provide you with the support of caring people. More importantly, the funeral is a way for you to mourn. If others tell you the funeral or other healing rituals such as these are silly or unnecessary, don't listen.

7. You have the right to embrace your spirituality.

If faith is a part of your life, express it in ways that seem appropriate to you. Allow yourself to be around people who understand and support your religious beliefs. If you feel angry at God, find someone to talk with who won't be critical of your feelings of hurt and abandonment.

8. You have the right to search for meaning.

You may find yourself asking, "Why did he or she die? Why this way? Why now?" Some of your questions may have answers, but some may not. And watch out for the clichéd responses some people may give you. Comments like, "It was God's will" or

"Think of what you have to be thankful for" are not helpful and you do not have to accept them.

9. You have the right to treasure your memories.

Memories are one of the best legacies that exist after the death of someone loved. You will always remember. Instead of ignoring your memories, find others with whom you can share them.

10. You have the right to move toward your grief and heal. Reconciling your grief will not happen quickly. Remember, grief is a process, not an event. Be patient and tolerant with yourself and avoid people who are impatient and intolerant with you. Neither you nor those around you must forget that the death of someone loved changes your life forever.

The Mourner's Bill of Rights by Alan D. Wolfelt, Ph.D., C.T.,

www.centerforloss.com,

https://www.centerforloss.com/wp-content/uploads/2016/02/MBR.pdf

Endnotes

Chapter One: My Winter Season

1. Carol A. Newsom, Jacqueline E. Lapsley, and Sharon H. Ringe, *The Women's Bible Commentary: Expanded Edition with Apocrypha/Deuterocanonical Books, and the New Testament* (Westminster: John Knox, 1998), 141.

2. Walter Brueggemann, *Spirituality of the Psalms*, (Minneapolis: Fortress Press, 2002), 14.

3. Nancy Reeves, PhD, *Found Through Loss: Healing Stories from Scripture and Everyday Sacredness*, (Kelowna, British Columbia: Northstone Publishing, 2003), 71.

4. Ibid, 71.

5. Leslie C. Allen, *A Liturgy of Grief: A Pastoral Commentary of Lamentations* (Grand Rapids, Michigan: Baker Academic, 2011), 24-25.

6. Timothy Keller, *Walking with God through Pain and Suffering* (New York: Penguin Books, 2013), 4-5.

7. Ellen F. Davis, *Getting Involved with God: Rediscovering the Old Testament* (Plymouth, UK: Cowley Publications, 2001), 121.

8. Genesis 6:6; Psalm 78:40, 58; Judges 10:16; Hosea 11:8-9; Isaiah 63:9-10.

9. John 16:33; 2 Timothy 1:8, 3:12; Luke 14:27; Psalm 34:19; 1 Peter 1:6-7, 4:12-13.

10. Ann Voskamp, *The Broken Way: a daring path into the abundant life* (Grand Rapids, Michigan: Zondervan, 2016), 17.

11. Ibid, 213.

12. Brené Brown, *Rising Strong* (New York: Spiegel & Grau, 2015), 50-51.

13. Davis, 122.

14. Robert Alter, *The Art of Biblical Poetry* (New York: Basic Books, 2011), 137.

15. Dallas Willard, *The Allure of Gentleness: Defending the Faith in the Manner of Jesus* (New York: Harper One, New York, 2016), 12.

16. Bible Project, *"The Book of Job"* (YouTube video), posted October 22, 2015, accessed October 15, 2019, https://www.youtube.com/watch?v=xQwnH8th_f.

Chapter Two: What the Book of Job Reveals about Suffering

1. E. Ray Clendenen, "The Message and Purpose of Job," *Academia Education,* accessed June 10, 2018, https://www.academia.edu/1926526/Message_and_Purpose_of_Job, 2.

2. Ibid, 2.

3. Bill T. Arnold and Bryan E. Beyer, *Encountering the Old Testament* (Grand Rapids, Michigan: Baker Books, 1999), 64. Diane Langberg, *Suffering and the Heart of God: How Trauma Destroys and Christ Restores* (Greensboro NC: New Growth Press, 2015), 49. Genesis 1-2.

4. Matthew 5:10; John 16:33; 2 Timothy 3:12.

5. Job 10:2-18, 16:6-17, 21:7-16, 19:21-22.

6. Tremper Longman III, Baker Commentary on the OT Wisdom and Psalms: *Job* (Grand Rapids, Michigan: Baker Academic, 2012), 89.

7. David J.A. Clines, World Biblical Commentary: *Job 1-20* (Grand Rapids, Michigan: Zondervan, 1989), 50.

8. Roger John Scholtz, "I Had Heard of You...but Now My Eye Sees You: Revisioning Job's Wife," Old Testament Essays. Authors of the articles, 2013, https://www.semanticscholar.org/paper/%22I-had-heard-of-you-.-.-.-but-now-my-eye-sees-you%22%3A-Scholtz/d5ee94001c41e50f8f27ca01f0eb950f3c01ad2c, accessed June 13, 2018, 1.

9. F. Rachel Magdalene, "Job's Wife as Hero: A Feminist-forensic Reading of the Book of Job, Biblical Interpretation," vol. 14, no. 3, Jan. 2006, The ATLA Serials (ATLAS®*)*, accessed June 7, 2018, https://www.academia.edu/1071737/2006_Jobs_Wife_as_Hero_A_Feminist-forensic_Reading_of_the_Book_of_Job, 214-215. And Daniel Darling, "The Most Misunderstood Woman in the Bible," *Today's Christian Woman*, 18 May 2011, accessed June 15, 2018, https://www.todayschristianwoman.com/site/utilities/print.html?type=article&id=92438, 1.

10. Longman, 90. And Clines, 51.

11. Clines, 52.

12. Ellen van Wolde, "The Development of Job: Mrs. Job as Catalyst in Feminist Companion to the Bible: 2nd Series 9," Edited by Athalya Brenner (Sheffield Academic Press, 2000), https://www.academia.edu/3546045/The_Development_of_Job_Mr.Job_as_Catalyst 204.

13. Newsom et al, 140.

14. Ibid, 140.

15. Ibid, 140.

Chapter Three: The Conversations

1. Clines, Job 1-2, 61-62.

2. Ibid, 63.

3. Ibid, 63.

4. Ibid, 63.

5. Health Television Network. *Spiritual Care Series, A Volunteer Training Course* (Baptist Housing; Delta, British Columbia, 2018), 69.

6. Arnold and Beyer, 147. Deuteronomy 28. 1 Chronicles 28:9.

7. H. Norman Wright, *Helping Those Who Hurt: Reaching Out to Your Friends in Need* (Minneapolis, Minnesota: Bethany House, 2003), 45.

8. Ibid, 45.

9. Rabbi Stephen B. Roberts, *Professional Spiritual and Pastoral Care: A Practical Clergy and Chaplain's Handbook* (Woodstock, Vermont: Skylight Paths Publishing, 2013), 5.

10. Ibid, 5.

11. Longman, 181.

12. Job 10:9, 17:16, 34:14-15, 40:13.

13. Timothy Keller, 119-120.

14. Gary R. Collins, Ph.D., *Christian Counseling: a Comprehensive Guide* (Nashville: Thomas Nelson, 2007), 467.

15. Hebrews 2:24, 9:15; 1 Timothy 2:5-6; Ephesians 1:19-20; Romans 8:34.

16. Luke 23:43, 24:1-47; 1 John 2:25, 5:11-13, 20; John 3:15-16, 6:40; Revelations 7:15-17, 21.

17. Timothy Keller, *On Death*, (United States: Penguin Books, 2020), 51, 53.

Chapter Four: A Framework for Loss and Grief

1. Collins, 466.

2. Scott Berinato, "That Discomfort You're Feeling is Grief," *Harvard Business Review*, March 23, 2020, https://hbr.org/amp/2020/03/that-discomfort-youre-feeling-is-grief, 3.

3. Ibid, 3.

4. Kenneth R. Mitchell and Herbert Anderson, *All Our Losses All Our Griefs: Resources for Pastoral Care* (Louisville, Kentucky: Westminster: John Knox Press, 1983), 18.

5. Ibid, 19.

6. Therese A. Rando, *Grief, Dying, and Death: Clinical Interventions for Caregiver* (Champaign, Illinois: Research Press, 1984), 43-57.

7. Ibid, 43.

8. Ibid, 47.

9. Ibid, 53.

10. Ibid, 16.

11. Collins, 472-475. Marney Thompson, RCC, "Providing a Safe Haven, An Attachment-Informed Approach to Grief Counselling," *Insights, The BC Association of Clinical Counsellors' Magazine*, Winter, 2018, 24. Roberts, 314.

12. Thompson, 25-27.

13. "Loss Grief Bereavement - BC Hospice and Palliative Care, Module Five," accessed August 1, 2019, https://bchpca.org/wp-content/uploads/Module-Five-Loss-Grief-Bereavement-Care.pdf., 5-11.

14. John W. James and Russell Friedman, *Grief Recovery Handbook: The Action Program for Moving Beyond Death, Divorce, and Other Losses* (New York: Collins Publishing, 2009), 11.

15. Angela Morrow, "The Four Phases and Tasks of Grief," verywellhealth.com, accessed August 3, 2019, https://www.verywellhealth.com/the-four-phases-and-tasks-of-grief-1132550, 1.

16. Allen, 20.

17. Robert W. Kellemen, *Spiritual Friends: A Methodology of Soul Care and Spiritual Direction* (Winona Lake, IN: BMH Books, 2005), 89.

18. Loss Grief Bereavement, 5.11.

19. Brueggemann, 8-11.

20. Ibid, 8.

21. Ibid, 8.

22. Ibid, 10.

23. Ibid, 10.

24. Ibid, 8

25. Ibid, 11.

Chapter Five: Basic Grief Reactions

1. "Loss Grief Bereavement, 5.12."

2. Reeves, 83.

3. Dr. William E. Hulme, *Christian Caregiving. Insights from the Book of Job* (St. Louis Concordia Publishing House, 1971), 10.

4. Donald Peel, *The Ministry of Listening: Team Visiting in Hospital and Home* (Toronto, Ontario: Anglican Book Centre, 1980), 45.

5. Clines, *Job 1-20*, 104.

6. Daniel Goleman, "Mourning. New Studies Affirm its Benefits," *The New York Times*, 5 Feb. 1985, accessed August 3, 2019, www.nytimes.com/1985/02/05/science/mourning-new-studies-affirm-its-benefits.html, 1.

7. Jill Anderson, *Thinking, Changing, Rearranging: Improving Self-Esteem in Young People* (Portland OR: Metamorphous Press, 1988), 6-7.

8. Ibid, 7.

9. Ibid, 7.

10. Paul David Tripp, *Instruments in the Redeemer's Hands: Helping People in Need of Change* (Phillipsburg, New Jersey: P & R Publishing, 2002), 197.

11. Ibid, 194-195.

Endnotes

12. Tula Karras, "Your Emotions: The Science of How You Feel," *National Geographic.* (Meredith Corporation: New York, NY, 2020), 63.

13. C. S. Lewis, *The Problem of Pain* (New York: Macmillan, Harper Collins Publishers, 1944), 93.

14. Goleman, 1.

15. Hulme, 31.

16. Emily Nagoski, Ph.D. and Amelia Nagoski, DMA, *Burnout: The Secret to Unlocking the Stress Cycle* (New York: Ballantine Books, 2019), 133-134.

17. Ibid, 124.

18. "Loss Grief Bereavement, 5.12."

19. Marlena Graves, *a beautiful disaster: finding hope in the midst of brokenness* (Grand Rapids, Michigan: Brazos Press, 2014), 50.

20. Spiritual Care Series, A Volunteer Training Course, 38.

21. Collins, 66.

22. Ibid, 66.

23. Clines, Vol. 17, xlii.

24. Ibid, xlvii.

25. Fr. Richard Rohr, "Stuck in the Body," *Center for Action and Contemplation*, February 20, 2020, https://cac.org/stuck-in-the-body-2020-02-20/?utm_source=cm&utm_medium=email&utm_campaign=dm&utm_content=summary, 1.

26. Ibid, 1.

27. Collins, 473.

28. Cari Romm, "Understanding How Grief Weakens the Body," *The Atlantic*, September 2014, https://www.theatlantic.com/health/archive/2014/09/understanding-how-grief-weakens-the-body/380006/, 1.

29. Ibid, 1.

30. Loss Grief Bereavement, 5:12.

Chapter Six: Consolation. Some Practical Responses

1. Spiritual Care Series, 68.

2. Collins, 68.

3. James E. Miller, *The Art of Listening in a Healing Way* (Fort Wayne, Indiana: Willowgreen Publishing, 2003), 37.

4. Ibid, 37.

5. Ibid, 51.

6. Peel, 34.

7. Miller, 53.

8. Longman, 449.

9. Hulme, 91-92.

10. Ibid, 91.

11. Ibid, 91.

12. Tripp, 156.

13. Ibid, 156.

14. Ibid, 157.

15. Ibid, 155-157.

16. Fr. Joseph Tham, "Communicating with Sufferers: Lessons From the Book of Job," *Academia Education,* https://www.academia.edu/8961063/Communicating_with_Suffere rs_Lessons_from_the_Book_of_Job, 7.

17. Ibid, 8.

18. Tripp, 131.

19. Peel, 14.

20. Ibid, 15.

21. Collins, 90.

22. Wright, 16.

Chapter Seven: Consolation. Some Theological Responses

1. John Patton, *Pastoral Care: An Essential Guide* (Nashville: Abingdon Press, 2015), 8.

2. Ibid, 9.

3. Derek Kidner, *The Wisdom of Proverbs, Job & Ecclesiastes* (Downers Grove, Illinois: Intervarsity Press, 1985), 61.

4. Rod J. K. Wilson, *How Do I Help a Hurting Friend?* (Vancouver, BC: Regent College Publishing, 2010), 64.

5. Keller, *Walking with God,* 216.

6. Patton, 47.

7. Gordon MacDonald, *Rebuilding Your Broken World* (Nashville: Oliver Nelson Books, 1988), 186.

8. Chandra Gunawan, "Retribution in the Wisdom Literature and Tradition," *Academic Education,*

https://www.academia.edu/11777072/Retribution_in_the_Wisdom _Literature_and_Tradition?email_work_card=interaction_paper, 1.

9. MacDonald, 189.

10. Ibid, 188.

11. Longman, 460.

12. Kidner, 72.

13. Soren Kierkegaard, *Christian Discourses,* trans. Walter Lowie (Oxford: Oxford University Press, 1940), *324.*

14. Tham, 6.

15. Ibid, 6.

16. Hulme, 105.

17. April Yamasaki, *Four Gifts: Seeking Self-Care for Heart, Soul, Mind and Strength* (Harrisonburg, Virginia: Herald Press, 2018, 62.

18. Wright, 140.

19. Keller, 287-288.

20. Ibid, 282-3.

21. Longman, 106.

22. Ibid, 106.

23. N.T. Wright, "Christianity Offers No Answers about the Coronavirus," *Time Magazine,* March 29, 2020, https://time.com/5808495/coronavirus-christianity/, 1.

24. Ibid, 1.

25. Rah, 21.

26. Ibid, 21.

27. Ibid, 21.

28. Nathaniel A. Carlson, "Lament: The Biblical Language of Trauma," *Academia Education*, Volume 11, Number 1, 2015, https://www.academia.edu/25374709/LAMENT_THE_BIBLICAL _LANGUAGE_OF_TRAUMA, 53.

29. Ibid, 54.

30. Ibid, 54.

31. Ibid, 62.

32. Longman, 106.

33. Ibid, 106.

Chapter Eight: Final Thoughts

1. Dan B. Allender, *The Healing Path: How the Hurts in Your Past can Lead You to a More Abundant Life* (Colorado Springs, Colorado: Waterbook Press, 1996), 4.

2. Ibid, 5.

3. Longman, 449.

4. Carol Meyers Editor, Toni Craven and Ross S. Kraemer, Associate Editors, *Women in Scripture: A Dictionary of Named and Unnamed Women in the Hebrew Bible, the Apocryphal/Deuterocanonical Books and the New Testament* (Grand Rapids, Michigan: William B. Eerdmans Publishing Company, 2000), 292.

5. Ibid, 292.

6. Karl G. Wilcox, "Job, his Daughters and his Wife," *Journal for the Study of the Old Testament*, Vol. 42.3 (2018), 314.

7. Longman, 451.

8. Peter Scazzero, *Emotionally Healthy Spirituality* (Nashville: Thomas Nelson, 2006), 129.

9. Ibid, 129.

10. Hulme, 105.

11. Longman, 452.

12. Ibid, 452.

13. Ibid, 452.

About The Author

Anne Mackie Morelli

Anne Mackie Morelli is a former member of the Canadian National Track and Field Team and Olympian, who is now a writer, educator, public speaker, and registered clinical counsellor. She is passionate about inspiring others to maximize their talents, strengths, and leadership abilities for the greater good. As a Christian, Anne strives to embody love by practicing restorative grace, compassion, inclusivity, and justice. She lives in British Columbia, Canada with Claudio, her husband of 44 years. They have three beloved sons and daughters-in-law, and four cherished grandsons. You can reach Anne at her website, Anne Mackie Morelli, www.annemackiemorelli.com, by email at anne@annemackiemorelli.com, on Twitter at @EAnneMorelli, or on Facebook @AnneMackieMorelliwriter

Manufactured by Amazon.ca
Bolton, ON

13889125R00136